HISTORIC MONUMENTS
OF NORTHERN IRELAND

1   Work in progress at Grey Abbey.

DEPARTMENT OF THE ENVIRONMENT
FOR NORTHERN IRELAND

Historic Monuments of Northern Ireland

AN INTRODUCTION AND GUIDE

BELFAST
HER MAJESTY'S STATIONERY OFFICE

Printed for Her Majesty's Stationery Office
by The Universities Press (Belfast) Ltd.

Dd. 8867752 C50 3/87

ISBN 0 337 08180 8

Contents

Folding map inside back cover

Preface

This guide goes to press at the end of the year in which we have been celebrating the centenary of the first Ancient Monuments Protection Act of 1882, though government involvement with monuments in Ireland goes back still further, to 1869. The guide covers 154 sites in State Care at the end of 1982, anticipating a few acquisition cases which are near completion, and lists over 250 other monuments. It replaces two volumes, *Ancient Monuments of Northern Ireland, volume I, In State Care*, and *volume II, Not in State Care*. The five editions of the *State Care* guide illustrate the progress of acquisitions: 22 sites in 1926, 27 in 1928, 50 in 1947, 67 in 1962 and 76 in 1966. Volume II appeared first in 1952 and consisted of an archaeological and historical introduction by Professor E M Jope and notes on selected sites. It was reissued in revised editions in 1963 and 1969. As I write at the end of 1982 the *State Care* guide is out of print and stocks of *Not in State Care* are running low.

The decision to produce an entirely new guide was made because the two earlier volumes, having done excellent service, are both considerably out of date. Some *Not* sites are now in State Care, 47 monuments were transferred to State Care from the county councils in 1973, and new sites are gradually passing into care year by year. Responsibility for Historic Monuments was transferred in 1976 from the Department of Finance to the Department of the Environment.

There will in future be no separate HMSO guide to monuments not in care. A general introduction, formerly a feature of the *Not in State Care* guide, is included in the present volume. Within the introduction State Care sites appear in bold type. The inventory of sites is arranged by county, the sites being grouped by period, numbered and identified on the folding map inside the back cover. Figures and plates are numbered continuously and these numbers appear in the margins. Whilst the amount of detail included on each site is sometimes less than in the 5th edition of the *State Care* guide, almost twice as many sites are covered and individual publications – official guides and guide-cards – are now available for some 25 sites. The lists of selected non-State Care sites are also arranged by counties with grid references and identification of period and type but no detail. Many of these are scheduled for protection under the Historic Monuments Act (NI) 1971. A general bibliography is given, as well as up-to-date references under individual site descriptions.

The guide owes a great deal to the work of the late Dudley Waterman, former Principal Inspector of Historic Monuments, and Pat Collins, retired Senior Inspector. Most of my colleagues in the Archaeological Survey have helped in compiling the guide (Nick Brannon, Hugh Dixon, Claire Foley, Chris Lynn, Marion Meek, Brian Williams and Mike Yates). Gail Pollock has been responsible for most of the photographic work, Philip Armstrong and Marion McLornan for the figures, and Emer O'Boyle for much editorial help.

ANN HAMLIN
December 1982

Abbreviations

Counties:
Ant Antrim; Arm Armagh; Ferm Fermanagh;
Ldy Londonderry; Tyr Tyrone.

Books and journals:
ASCD, An archaeological survey of county Down (HMSO, Belfast, 1966).
Co Louth Archaeol J, Journal of the County Louth Archaeological Society.
Gwynn and Hadcock 1970, A Gwynn and R N Hadcock, *Medieval religious houses: Ireland* (London, 1970).
Hayes-McCoy 1964, G A Hayes-McCoy, *Ulster and other Irish maps c.1600* (Dublin, 1964).
Hickey 1976, H Hickey, *Images of stone: figure sculpture of the Lough Erne basin* (Belfast, 1976).
J Roy Soc Antiq Ireland, Journal of the Royal Society of Antiquaries of Ireland.
PSAMNI, A preliminary survey of the ancient monuments of Northern Ireland (HMSO, Belfast, 1940).
Proc Belfast Nat Hist Phil Soc, Proceedings of the Belfast Natural History and Philosophical Society.
Proc Roy Irish Acad, Proceedings of the Royal Irish Academy.
Ulster J Archaeol, Ulster Journal of Archaeology.

Miscellaneous:
m metre, km kilometre.
DOENI, Department of the Environment for Northern Ireland.
HMSO, Her Majesty's Stationery Office.

Illustrations

Figures and plates are numbered continuously. The number appears in the margin beside a reference to the site in the text. All the drawings and photographs are Crown Copyright Reserved unless otherwise indicated. The figures are by Philip Armstrong and Marion McLornan except for 44 (Stephen Shaw) and 123 (Robin Carson). Most of the Crown Copyright photographs are by Gail Pollock and A E P Collins. Number 132 is Crown Copyright, reproduced with permission from the Ministry of Defence. Numbers 22, 28, 98 and 135 are Copyright University of Cambridge Committee for Aerial Photography. We are grateful to all the individuals and bodies whose copyright material is reproduced.

County Antrim

County Armagh

County Down

County Fermanagh

County Londonderry

Access to Monuments

Most State Care sites are open at all times, but a few with caretakers have limited opening hours or are closed because of work in progress. Since these arrangements are subject to change they are not included in the guide. To be sure of access and to arrange for group admissions please contact Historic Monuments and Buildings Branch at Calvert House, 23 Castle Place, Belfast BT1 1FY. Some of the sites which came recently into care are not yet conserved or presented, but progress on these is made each year. For access to monuments not in State Care please see page 148.

A Warning

Searching for archaeological material by digging without an excavation licence, whether as a result of using a metal detector or in any other way, is strictly illegal under the Historic Monuments Act (NI) 1971.

Introduction

PREHISTORIC MONUMENTS

The first clear evidence of man in Ireland comes from the MESOLITHIC
PERIOD after the end of the last Ice Age, from about 7000 bc.* Whatever
land bridges may once have linked Ireland with Britain had been submerged
by the sea, and the first settlers must have arrived in boats from somewhere
on the western shores of Britain. They lived by hunting wild animals and
birds, fishing, and collecting shell fish, nuts, wild fruits, roots and leaves.
The presence of Mesolithic people can be detected from the debris of this
food collecting and especially from their distinctive flint implements and the
waste from their manufacture.

The earliest structures associated with Mesolithic man in Ireland were
discovered by excavation close to the later mound in **Mount Sandel**
townland, about 1¼ miles (2 km) upstream from Coleraine (Ldy). Groups
of post-holes, pits and hearths suggested the existence of circular huts about
6 metres in diameter. In and around them were thousands of pieces of
worked flint, much of it waste material but including many microliths, tiny
finished implements which probably served as heads and barbs for wooden
arrows for hunting and fishing. Larger stone tools were used in wood-
working, for making huts, boats, fish-traps and bows. Food remains,
including burned bones of mammals, birds and fish, and many hazel nut
shells suggested that the site was occupied both in summer and throughout
the winter. Radiocarbon dates range from about 7000 to 6500 bc.

Mesolithic flint material has been found in other parts of the Bann valley and
in coastal areas of Antrim and Down as well as on the shores of Lough
Neagh and Lough Macnean (Ferm). Radiocarbon dates suggest a long
time-span for this hunting/gathering economy, from 7000 to 3500 or 3000
bc, continuing even after the arrival of the first farming settlers.

The NEOLITHIC PERIOD began soon after 4000 bc and saw the first settled
farming communities established in Ireland. The first farmers in the north

---

* The use in the text of lower-case bc, following current practice, indicates a date established
  by radiocarbon measurement based on a half-life for radiocarbon of 5560 years. Upper-case
  BC or AD with radiocarbon dates indicate calibrated dates, adjusted by a correction factor
  based on dendrochronology (tree-ring dating). Elsewhere BC and AD indicate calendar years,
  unconnected with radiocarbon dating.

1

may have come from Britain, perhaps across the North Channel, bringing seed-corn and young livestock (cattle, pigs and sheep or goats) in their boats. A settled farming regime allowed some industrial specialisation and also the building of substantial, long-lasting structures. The Neolithic period continued to about 1800 bc, a span of at least two thousand years, and the sites surviving from this long period include settlements, industrial sites and, most obvious in the landscape, different types of stone-built tombs.

Settlements leave little or no surface trace and are therefore difficult to find. The most informative Neolithic settlement site yet excavated in Ulster was on a small glacial sand and gravel hill at Ballynagilly (Tyr), now quarried away. Here traces of a substantial timber-built house were found, rectangular in plan and dated by radiocarbon to 3200 bc. Groupings of post- and stake-holes have been found associated with Neolithic material in the Dundrum sandhills (Down), and other Neolithic settlement sites have been identified from local concentrations of worked flint and potsherds turned up during cultivation. Excavation of sites recognised from surface finds could well produce more Neolithic house plans and other evidence of occupation.

Most of our knowledge of Neolithic *industrial activity* centres round the exploitation of stone resources. The chalk exposed in the cliffs at the edges of the Antrim plateau contains plentiful supplies of flint nodules which could be collected as beach pebbles, or fresh flint could be quarried from the chalk. Opencast workings have been identified at Black Mountain overlooking Belfast and on Ballygalley Hill north of Larne (both Ant). Nowhere else in the highland zone of the British Isles is there such an abundance of good quality flint for making sharp-edged tools and weapons. Flint was supplemented by porcellanite, a hard, tough, bluish-grey metamorphic rock, ideal for axe manufacture. This was extracted from outcrops in the Antrim basalt at Tievebulliagh near Cushendall and Brockley on Rathlin Island, and roughly chipped on the site to the shape of axe and adze blades. These 'rough-outs' then seem to have been carried away for finishing elsewhere by grinding and polishing. Porcellanite is such a rare and distinctive material that it is almost certain that any porcellanite blade found in the British Isles came originally from a county Antrim source, and Antrim products are therefore well-attested as far afield as Aberdeenshire, Dorset and Kent.

Megalithic tombs, built of large stones, are the most prominent and best-studied Neolithic field monuments. These tombs are found in the Mediterranean region, the Atlantic coasts and islands of western Europe and in Scandinavia, and several different types are recognised in Ireland. Prominent in the north is the *court grave* (also known as court cairn, horned cairn and court tomb). These were entered through a semicircular forecourt at the wider end of a long cairn, somewhat wedge-shaped in plan. From the

2

2, 3   Annaghmare Court Grave (Arm) during excavation: view of burial gallery from court; below, view of court showing post-and-panel construction.

3

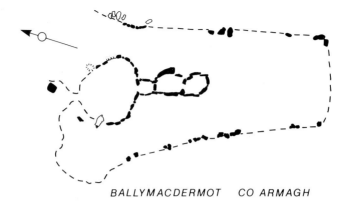

BALLYMACDERMOT CO ARMAGH

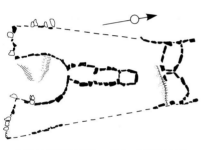

ANNAGHMARE CO ARMAGH

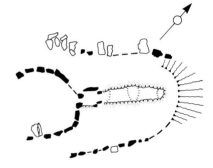

DOOEY'S CAIRN CO ANTRIM

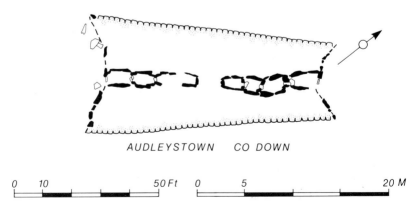

AUDLEYSTOWN CO DOWN

4 *Plans of Court Graves (black stones* in situ, *white stones disturbed).*

court opened a burial gallery, divided by horizontal stones or pairs of jamb   2
stones into two or more segments. The side walls were built of large stones
set on edge and the roof was of lintels or corbelling, or a mixture of the two.
Lintels are long stones spanning the whole width of the gallery whilst a
corbelled roof is formed by setting each course of stones slightly overhanging the one below until the gap is so narrow that it can be bridged by a single
stone. The long sides of the cairn were usually supported by a kerb or
retaining wall. The curved forecourt façade was sometimes built in a
'post-and-panel' technique, with widely-spaced uprights joined by panels of
dry-stone walling, seen especially well at **Annaghmare** (Arm). Extra room   3
for burials was achieved by building double-ended cairns (dual court   87
graves) as at **Audleystown** (Down) and **Ballybriest** (Ldy), or lateral cham-   118
bers entered from the cairn's long sides, as at **Cregganconroe** (Tyr). Both   128
inhumation and cremation burials have been found in excavated court
graves, and a mixture of the two. Finds include hand-made pottery, flint
implements and stone beads. More than 300 court graves are known in
Ireland and their distribution is markedly northern, north of a line from
Louth to Mayo. Similar graves are found in south-west Scotland: **Dooey's
Cairn** (Ant) is very closely paralleled in Scotland.   72

Another type of megalith tomb, widespread in Wales and Cornwall as well
as Ireland, is the *portal grave* (portal tomb or portal dolmen). This was   6
usually a single burial chamber, roofed with one huge capstone poised on
two tall uprights and sloping down towards a back-stone. The entrance
('portal') was often closed by a large slab set between the uprights, rather
like a door, well seen at **Ballykeel** (Arm). Here the stone chamber is at one   5

5   *Ballykeel Dolmen (Arm), portal grave.*

end of a long cairn, but usually the cairn (if it existed) has been removed and the 'skeleton' of the stone grave is all that remains, seen most spectacularly at **Legananny** (Down). Huge capstones can be seen at **Goward** and **Kilfeaghan** (Down), and other fine examples are the Kempe Stones near Dundonald and Slidderyford Dolmen near Dundrum (both Down). Over 150 portal graves are known in Ireland, many of them in the same northern area as the court graves, but extending also further south-east.

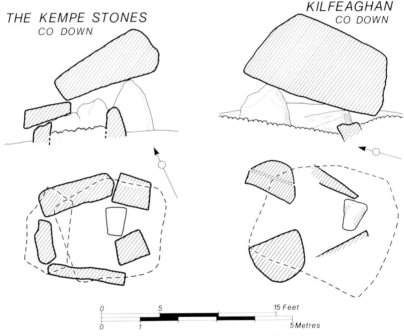

THE KEMPE STONES
CO DOWN

KILFEAGHAN
CO DOWN

6 *Portal Graves: sections and elevations above, plans below.*

Largest and most spectacular of the Neolithic graves in Ireland are *passage graves*, in which a burial chamber in a circular mound was reached by a passage. The walls of chamber and passage could be built of upright slabs or of massive dry-walling. Passages were roofed with lintels and led into a chamber, circular, rectangular, polygonal or cruciform in plan, usually roofed by corbelling. The finest Irish passage graves are in the Boyne Valley, at New Grange, Knowth and Dowth (Meath). Excavation suggests a date for these round about 2500 bc, though the simpler monuments at Carrowmore (Sligo) seem to have been built before 3000 bc. The largest northern passage graves so far identified are the Belmore Mountain cairn (Ferm) and the excavated south cairn high on **Slieve Gullion** (Arm). Another large example once crowned the summit of Slieve Donard, highest peak of the Mourne Mountains, at over 2700 feet. Somewhat unusual is the

6

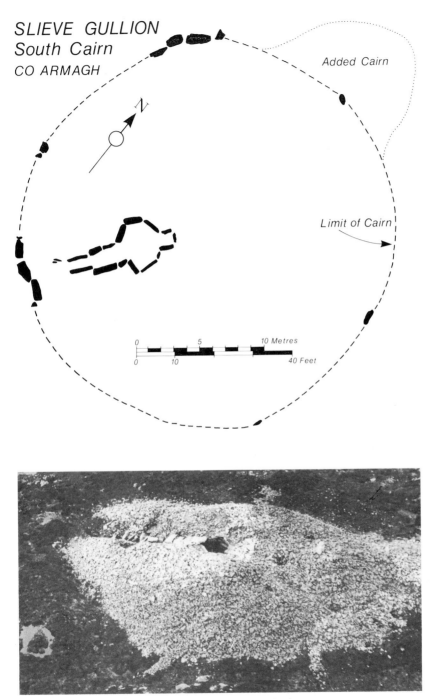

SLIEVE GULLION
South Cairn
CO ARMAGH

Added Cairn

N

Limit of Cairn

| 0 | | 5 | | 10 Metres |
| 0 | 10 | | | 40 Feet |

7, 8   *Slieve Gullion South Cairn (Arm), plan and air view.*

fine hilltop grave at **Knockmany** (Tyr) where the monument has all the features of a passage grave except the passage! Passage graves sometimes occur in groups and the main northern concentrations are in the Clogher Valley and in north-east Antrim.

The **Slieve Gullion** passage grave is undecorated, but a feature of the sites at
129 **Knockmany** and Sess Kilgreen (Tyr) and the Carnanmore cairn (Ant) is pecked or incised decoration on the stones. This could be curvilinear – spirals, concentric circles, multiple arcs – and rectilinear, including zig-zags, triangles and lozenges. The burial deposit in passage graves was usually cremated bone, and where unburned bones have been found they can generally be explained as insertions of the Bronze Age. Distinctively decorated pottery bowls (called Carrowkeel Ware after the site in Sligo) have been found during excavations, also skewer-like bone pins and stone beads and pendants.

Not fitting readily into any class is the complex burial monument at **Millin**
9 **Bay** (Down), excavated in 1953 and datable from its admittedly sparse finds to the late Neolithic. The site appears now as a sandy, grass-grown mound with the tips of some stones visible, but excavation uncovered a long burial cist, a slab-lined compartment, with the bones of fifteen individuals, the skeletons taken to pieces and neatly stacked, with surrounding stone set-tings and further cists. Many of the stones were decorated with incised and pecked motifs in the tradition of passage grave art. Perhaps a newly-arrived

9   Millin Bay Cairn (Down) during excavation in 1953.

group built this unusual structure for the accumulated bones of their revered ancestors brought from elsewhere?

Whilst many megalithic monuments can be classed easily into types, in other cases it can be difficult to decide on the type without excavation. **Annadorn Dolmen** (Down) looks rather like a portal grave, but earlier accounts indicate that it may be the remains of a passage grave, and it has been suggested that **Ballylumford Dolmen** (Ant) was originally a passage 71 grave rather than a portal grave. The covering cairn at **Creggandevesky** (Tyr) was so well preserved that the site could not be classified more closely than 'long cairn', but excavation from 1979 to 1982 showed it to be an exceptionally intact court grave still enveloped in its cairn. At the other extreme, it is only through early 19th-century engravings that we know the two stones in a hedge at Annacloghmullin (Arm) to be the remains of a once impressive court grave.

Megaliths have for so long been prominent features in the Irish landscape that it is not surprising stories have grown up around them. They have been seen as beds (Dermot and Grania's Bed, Loughmacrory, Tyr), as Giants' Graves (**Lisky**, Tyr) or Druids' Altars (**Churchtown** and **Glenknock**, Tyr). The name 'Cloghogle' or 'Cloghtogle' is common for portal graves (from Irish 'high stone'), for example the fine roadside monument at Tamlaght (Ldy) near Coagh. Local names include the King's Ring for **Clontygora** 79 court grave and the Black Castle for the site at **Annaghmare** (both Arm). 2, 3 The name **Ossian's Grave** (Ant) for the beautifully sited court grave inland 73 from Cushendall may be no earlier than the 18th century, when the Scottish writer MacPherson popularised the heroic tales of Ossian. **Dooey's Cairn** 72 (Ant) is named from the family who so generously placed the monument in State Care in 1976.

Towards the end of the Neolithic period a new impressive type of field monument appears in the archaeological record. In addition to large funerary structures like the passage graves, energy, organisation and resources were turned to other ambitious projects. The large, circular, embanked structures known as *henges*, like the **Giant's Ring** near Belfast, were prob- 89 ably made and used late in the third millennium BC. The precise function of these sites remains uncertain, but they may have been substantial 'public' monuments, providing focal points for meetings, markets or other social gatherings.

Metalworking in Ireland began around 2000 BC, and at the same time distinctive new styles of pottery came into use and different burial practices were adopted. It has often been claimed that immigrants from Britain and

9

the Continent were responsible for these changes, but more importance is now attached to indigenous development. Many of the characteristic features of the earlier BRONZE AGE seem to have their origins in the late Neolithic, and the distinction between the two periods is not very clearly defined.

11   This is well illustrated by another type of megalithic tomb, the *wedge grave*. A small oval or heel-shaped cairn covered a simple elongated burial chamber, entered most frequently from the south-west, sometimes through a small antechamber. The burial gallery was usually made of large upright stones and roofed with lintels. Becoming narrower and lower towards the rear, the gallery has the characteristic wedge-shaped plan and profile which give the type its name.

Over 400 wedge graves have been identified in Ireland and they are largely confined to western areas. In the north the main concentrations occur in Londonderry, Tyrone and Fermanagh, with a few outliers in Antrim. Examples at **Ballygroll** and **Ballybriest** (Ldy) are in State Care, and other 10, 11   fine sites can be seen at Loughmacrory (Tyr), Dunteige (Ant), Boviel and Largantea (Ldy). Of the few wedge graves which have been excavated, several have produced fragments of the distinctive 'beaker' style of pottery, datable to the very beginning of the Bronze Age, but there can be no doubt that wedge graves continue the megalithic burial traditions seen in the court graves and portal graves of the Neolithic.

In the late third and early second millennia BC a general movement can be

10   Boviel Wedge Grave (Ldy).

LOUGHMACRORY CO TYRONE

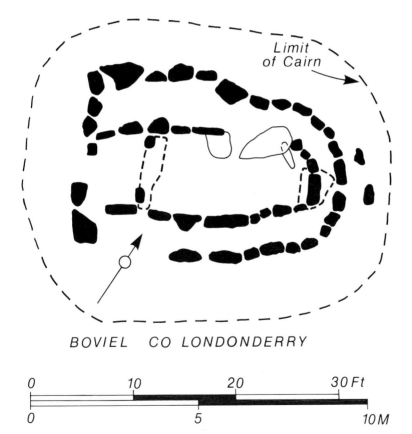

Limit
of Cairn

BOVIEL CO LONDONDERRY

| 0 | | 10 | | 20 | | 30 Ft |
| 0 | | | 5 | | | 10 M |

11 *Plans of Wedge Graves.*

traced away from multiple burial in the accessible vaults of chambered tombs and more importance seems to have been attached to the individual burial deposit. The types of burial site, and the burial rite itself, were extremely varied in the Bronze Age. The body was sometimes buried, but cremation was more usual. The burned remains were often placed in a distinctive cinerary urn, but they could also be set in a hole in the ground and covered with an inverted pottery vessel. Frequently, however, no urn has been found and the remains must have been deposited in a bag or box of perishable material, long since decayed. Both inhumed and cremated remains might be placed in a *short cist*, a closed stone 'box', sunk into the ground. The burial was sometimes accompanied by a pottery vessel, originally perhaps holding an offering. Simple items like beads or bone pins could be deposited with the body, but in a few cases more valuable objects have been found. Bronze daggers, fragments of gold and necklaces of jet and amber may point to the wealth and importance of the dead individual.

Considerable care could be lavished on a single burial. A domed mound of earth – a *round barrow* – or of stones – a *round cairn* – was sometimes built, as a prominent and lasting grave marker. Like the earlier passage graves, these were often sited in dominant positions in the landscape, for example at Largantea (Ldy) and near the summit of **Slieve Gullion** (Arm). Other Bronze Age burial monuments were less conspicious. Burials could be clustered together, often on a small natural mound or hillock, to form a *flat*

12 Bronze Age stone cist with pot, skull and other bones, at Stranagalwilly (Tyr).

13   Slieve Gullion North Cairn (Arm).

cemetery, like the excavated site at Cloghskelt (Down). Although there may originally have been visible structures or grave markers, perhaps of wood, there are now rarely any surface traces.

Bronze Age man also made use of earlier monuments for burial. It seems that Neolithic chambered tombs retained their funerary associations well into the second millennium BC: Bronze Age burials have been found in the fabric of Neolithic long cairns, and there are even examples of Bronze Age burials within the chambers of some Neolithic graves. A swelling in the outline of the cairn of **Slieve Gullion** (Arm) passage grave may mark the position of an added Bronze Age round cairn.

7

The ritual and spiritual life of the earlier Bronze Age may also be reflected in the *stone circles and alignments* which cluster so markedly in mid Ulster, especially around the Sperrin Mountains. The stones are often quite small, and when peat has subsequently grown they can be obscured from view. Though easily recognised during turf-cutting by hand, such buried features are particularly vulnerable to damage during mechanical peat-cutting or land reclamation with heavy machinery.

Although the stones are rarely of impressive size, the extent and complexity of some sites are remarkable. At **Beaghmore** (Tyr) seven stone circles, ten alignments of stones and over a dozen cairns were revealed as the covering peat was removed. Other sites, like **Drumskinny** (Ferm), are less extensive

14
127
112

13

14   Beaghmore Stone Circles, Cairns and Alignments (Tyr).

but show the same care in their organisation. The interpretation of these impressive but enigmatic monuments remains uncertain. They clearly involved a great deal of work, both in planning and construction, and must have been important to their Bronze Age builders. The stones seem to have been positioned with some reference to the seasons, the sun or the moon, but not necessarily with any high degree of precision. To describe them as ritual structures clearly evades many questions, but within the present limits of our knowledge this is all that can be said with confidence.

15   Isolated *standing stones* are found throughout Ireland, and are perhaps the simplest of all the types of monuments, yet they are difficult to date and

15   Ballard Standing Stone (Arm).

place in a cultural or chronological context. They may have been set up over a long period and for different purposes. They can even be difficult to identify certainly as antiquities: recent cattle-rubbing stones and glacial erratics have been mistaken for ancient standing stones. A group of standing stones, or even a single stone, can be the last surviving remains of a once larger monument: for example the one stone on the hillside at **Mobuy** (Ldy) is said to have been part of the 'Druids Circle'. Despite these problems, there remains a large class of probably prehistoric standing stones, clearly in the strong Irish megalithic tradition. Excavations have tended to support a Bronze Age date and have shown that some marked the site of burials, but others did not. They could have marked routes or boundaries or the site of notable events: many explanations are possible. There are standing stones in State Care at **Duncarbit**, inland from Ballycastle (Ant), and at **Tattykeel, Grange** and **Berrysfort** (all Tyr).

A small class of *decorated stones* may also date from the Bronze Age. The decoration consists mainly of hollows (cup-marks), circles and concentric circles, sometimes linked by long curving lines These motifs were normally carved, or more accurately 'pecked', on to rock outcrops or large boulders, as at Ballystokes (Down) and Reyfad (Ferm). Occasionally a slab covering a   16 cist may have similar markings: examples are recorded at Glenmakeeran (Ant) and in Loughermore Forest (Ldy). Although some of the motifs are similar to those associated with passage graves, the Bronze Age style is quite distinct.

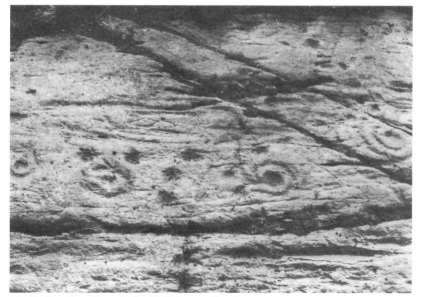

16   Ballystokes (Down), detail of decorated rock outcrop.

15

As in the Neolithic period, Bronze Age *settlement sites* are elusive, and most of our information is inevitably derived from burial and ritual monuments. The excavations at Ballynagilly (Tyr) did, however, reveal evidence for domestic activity associated with early Bronze Age pottery of the 'beaker' type, and early Bronze Age round houses were identified at Downpatrick. Later Bronze Age occupation has also been recognised at Downpatrick, on Cathedral Hill, and circular house foundations of the same general period have been found below the mound on the hilltop at **Navan Fort** (Arm). With such limited evidence our understanding of everyday life in the Bronze Age is slight, and we must look to future fieldwork and excavation to broaden our knowledge.

Many Bronze Age monuments are sited in upland areas which are now agriculturally barren and to our eyes thoroughly inhospitable. It may seem puzzling that such country was favoured by prehistoric man, but the climate in the second millennium BC was warmer and drier than today. Much of the landscape had a heavy tree cover, and the light, well-drained, thinly-wooded upland soils may have been particularly suitable for early agriculture. It is even possible that forest clearance and cultivation at this early date contributed to the deterioration in upland soil fertility, and ultimately to the onset of peat formation.

The discovery of bronze and the development of metalworking skills have long been recognised as the major technological achievement of the period. In Ireland a high standard of craftsmanship was maintained, in the use of gold as well as bronze. Gold neck ornaments (lunulae and torcs), ear-rings, clothes fasteners, pendants and arm bands have been found, all carefully made and often finely decorated. Bronze was also used for personal items but it seems to have been especially valuable for functional objects like axes, sickles and knives, replacing to some extent the less efficient stone tools of Neolithic times. Weapons are prominent, beginning with simple knives and daggers and developing into a comprehensive armoury of halberds, spears, rapiers and swords.

The archaeological evidence for the Irish IRON AGE, from 300–200 BC to 400 AD, is still relatively scarce and few field monuments can reliably be assigned to the Iron Age. This obscurity is puzzling since the period immediately precedes the time of the first written records in Ireland and it is often claimed that the earliest Irish sagas look back to the Iron Age. It is likely that the knowledge of iron-working reached Ireland through immigrants, perhaps craftsmen, warriors, or other settlers from Britain, who also introduced a vigorous new decorative art applied to bronze objects. The monuments characteristic of the Iron Age in Britain and on the Continent are, however, uncommon in Ireland: hillforts, small enclosed farmsteads, barrows and flat cemeteries, and temples, sometimes with ritual shafts or pits. It seems that late Bronze Age Ireland may have been much less affected than Britain by cultural influences, and indeed immigrants, from the Continent.

One recognisably Iron Age element is the art style known as La Tène, after an important site in Switzerland. This decoration is found on a small number of objects in Ireland, almost all 'stray finds' (not from excavated sites), including sword scabbards, horse bits and ornaments. La Tène decoration is also occasionally found on bone and stone, and a fine Iron Age decorated stone has been recognised, built into the angle of the ruined church at Derrykeighan (Ant). The double-sided figure on Boa Island (Ferm) is unparalleled in Ireland but by Continental analogy is probably of Iron Age date.

17   Boa Island Figure (Ferm).

18, 19   Navan Fort (Arm) during excavation:
above, the cairn; below, wooden structures under the cairn.

18

Navan Fort, west of Armagh city, was the legendary Ulster capital in the early sagas (*Eamhain Macha*). It appears now as a huge circular hilltop enclosure, 375 metres in diameter. The massive bank is outside, downslope from, the wide ditch. Excavations from 1963 to 1971 showed that the large mound in the interior covered a cairn which encased the posts of a wooden structure, 40 metres in diameter, which was probably built, deliberately buried and burned in the Iron Age.

Another northern monument now firmly dated to this period is the Dorsey, a large, irregularly-shaped enclosure at Drummill Bridge in south Armagh. The enclosure measures about 0·8 km north-south by 1·6 km from north-east to south-west, defined by banks and ditches and piled structures across wet ground. It embraces varied terrain – ridges, rocky outcrops and bogs – and seems designed to block an important route northwards into Ulster. The monument is unique, and its date has long been a puzzle, but recent excavation has introduced some certainty. Dendrochronology has shown, by matching the tree-rings of Dorsey wood piles with Navan Fort timbers, that the wood for the two sites was cut at about the same time, probably in about 100 BC.

Several lengths of *linear earthworks* in Down and Armagh, known locally as the Dane's Cast, may have been built in the Iron Age but are not yet closely dated. One length, about a mile long, crosses the same route as the Dorsey, some 4 miles (6·5 km) south-east of Navan Fort. A longer stretch survives discontinuously for about 5 miles (8 km) east and south of Scarva (Down) and another, shorter, section can be traced east of Killevy in south Armagh.

20   The Dorsey Enclosure (Arm), air view of south-west area.

These are often impressive monuments but are difficult to preserve and make easily accessible because of their extent through private grounds and farmland.

Another type of field monument which may prove to belong to the Iron Age is the *ring-barrow*, usually consisting of a cremation burial in a flat central space or a low mound about 5 metres in diameter, surrounded by a continuous shallow ditch, with a correspondingly low bank outside. A ring-barrow stands in the south end of the hillfort at Clogher (Tyr). Iron Age cremation burials were inserted into the Neolithic passage grave in Kiltierney deerpark (Ferm), when it was already some 2000 years old. Small objects typical of the Iron Age accompanied the cremations, including a glass bead and bronze fibula or 'safety-pin' brooch.

EARLY CHRISTIAN PERIOD MONUMENTS

Though Ireland was never invaded by the Romans, it is clear that there were many contacts with Britain during the four centuries of Roman rule there. These contacts must have taken many forms, including trade, settlement, marriage, gift-giving, slavery, mercenary service and raiding, and there is growing evidence that the contacts contributed towards the economic revitalization and expansion which can be traced from about 400 AD.

The use of the term 'Early Christian' is well established in Ireland for the period from about 400 AD to the changes of the 12th century. It can be criticised for emphasising only one aspect of a complex culture and alternatives suggested and sometimes used include 'Early Historic', based on the first occurrence of written sources, 'Early Medieval', and 'Later Iron Age', after the Scandinavian pattern. But since there is not yet any unanimity over an alternative, we retain the term Early Christian for the period from about 400 AD to the 12th century.

The *secular settlements* of Early Christian Ireland are those of the grades of society described in the early law tracts and glimpsed in other written sources: of the kings, royal and noble families, of free land-owning classes and of unfree labouring peoples. Though there is evidence for persistent small-scale, local instability, expressed in raiding and petty warfare, settled life seems to have continued without major upheavals for many centuries. Even the impact of the fierce Vikings was limited, and no type of Viking field monument in Ireland has yet been detected. Settlement sites from this long period are numerous, totalling tens of thousands in the whole of

Ireland, and they contain a unique store of information about a rich culture, archaic in structure but open and receptive to new trends and influences. The range of settlement sites includes raths, cashels, crannogs, promontory forts, open settlements and souterrains.

Most numerous are the enclosed farmsteads known as *raths* (or *ring-forts*). 21 The total for all Ireland has been estimated to be some 30 to 40,000 (probably an *under*-estimate) and raths are by far the most common and characteristic monuments of the Irish countryside. In some areas, like south Antrim, they occur as frequently as modern farms. They have given their name to many townlands – *rath* and especially *lis* are common elements in townland names – but in the countryside they are universally known as 'forts'.

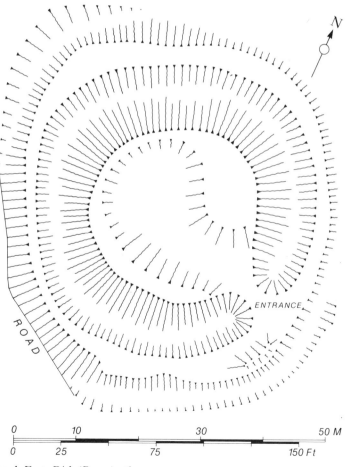

21   *Rough Fort, Risk (Down), plan.*

A 'typical' rath would have a circular open space some 35 metres in diameter, surrounded by a bank perhaps 4 metres wide and 2 metres high, with an enclosing ditch crossed by a causeway to an entrance gap. Often the interior sloped down towards the entrance to aid drainage, and interior features may include a souterrain (see further below) and traces of house sites, visible as slightly raised irregular platforms. But there are many permutations on this 'typical' appearance, with differing sizes and shapes, multiplication of banks and ditches, adaptation of natural defensive features, and later disturbances. The most common variant is the 'platform rath', where the ditch spoil instead of forming an enclosing bank was spread over the whole interior to create a low platform, one metre or less in height. Another variant is the 'raised rath', where prolonged occupation and deliberate heightening have created a substantial mound, perhaps as much as 4 metres high. These are sometimes difficult to distinguish without excavation from later Anglo-Norman castle mounds.

Few 'ordinary' raths are in State Care, partly because they *are* so common, but a good example can be seen at the roadside near Moira, **Rough**
21 **Fort**, Risk (Down). Amongst the largest and most spectacular sites are
22 **Lisnagade** and **Lisnavaragh** (Down), with three enclosing banks and ditches. It is possible that the multiplication of banks and ditches, of little extra defensive value, was an indicator of the prestige and labour resources of the occupant. Perhaps the most elaborate of all is Dunglady (Ldy), with four defensive rings, where the enclosed central area is tiny compared with

22   Lisnagade (Down), air view of trivallate rath and attached small rath.

22

the massive defences. Raths occasionally occur in pairs or small groups, sometimes touching, as at Ballypalady, Ballykennedy and Tully (all Ant).

Most of our information about the date and purpose of raths comes from excavation, and over 50 examples in Northern Ireland have been excavated for research or in advance of destruction. Some scholars argue for prehistoric – Iron Age or even earlier – origins for the type, but the northern evidence argues strongly for the Early Christian period: the great majority of excavated sites can be dated to the period 500-1100 AD. Excavation has often uncovered a farmstead with a house, of wattles, planks, stone, mud or sods, sometimes with outbuildings. A recently excavated rath at **Ballywee** 23
(Ant) produced a wide range of evidence. The relatively slight encircling

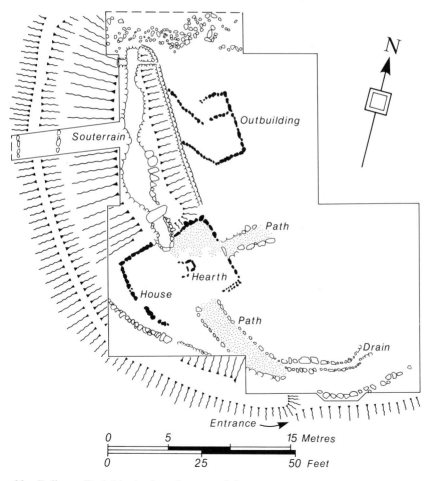

23   Ballywee Rath (Ant), plan of excavated features.

earthworks served mainly to deflect surface water from the occupied area, 60 metres in diameter, with a second smaller enclosure adjoining to the north-west. To the left of the undefended entrance a paved path with kerbs and a drain led to a rectangular stone-paved house, approached also by a cobbled path from the north-east. At the back was the entrance to a souterrain, and elsewhere in the enclosure were two more souterrains and three outbuildings. Finds of pottery and domestic rubbish were concentrated around the house and sparse elsewhere.

Finds from excavated sites indicate a settled mixed agricultural economy: animal bones, querns for grinding grain, coarse hand-made pottery known as 'souterrain ware' (north-east Ulster seems to have been the only part of Ireland where pottery vessels were commonly made in this period), spindle whorls, iron knives and axes, and personal ornaments including beads, pins and armlets – but hardly ever weapons. In wet conditions wood can survive, like the churn excavated at **Lissue** (Ant), also leather and other organic materials.

24 Another type of enclosure, the *cashel*, is broadly similar to raths in date and

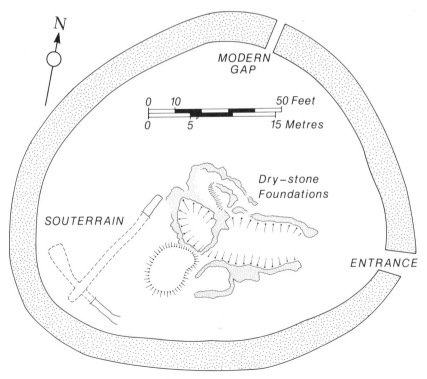

24   *Drumena Cashel (Down), plan.*

function but is entirely stone-built and rarely has a ditch. Much less common than raths, cashels tend to occur in rocky upland areas where stone is plentiful and ditch-digging difficult. Circular or oval in plan, the surrounding wall is dry-built of rubble and is very thick (2-3 metres) in proportion to its height (perhaps 2 metres). Outer and inner faces are carefully built, often with noticeably larger stones in the lower courses, but the wall core is of dumped rubble. When badly ruined the wall faces can be completely covered with fallen rubble and the whole wall appears as a bank of stones. Recent sheepfolds and other animal enclosures can superficially resemble cashels, but the walls of the modern enclosures are usually much thinner and more irregular. Excavated cashels tend to produce the same features and finds as raths, though stone was of course the favoured material for houses and other internal structures. A good example near Castlewellan is **Drumena** (Down), partly reconstructed after some excavation in the 24, 25 1920s. In the interior are a small T-shaped souterrain and some rather jumbled house foundations. Another good example, with a length of passage in the wall thickness, is at Altagore near Cushendun (Ant). The cashel at Drumaroad (Down), White Fort, was excavated in the 1960s and produced the foundation of a squarish stone and mud house.

Absent from Northern Ireland are the massive, spectacular cashels of the west coast like Staigue (Kerry), Dun Oengus (Inishmore, Aran Islands) and Grianan of Aileach (Donegal). There is a body of opinion that sees these as Iron Age in date, but there is no doubt that the datable northern cashels of

25   *Drumena Cashel (Down) from the south.*

modest size belong, like the excavated raths, to the Early Christian period. We can, however, note one cashel of unusual size in an ecclesiastical 31 context: **Nendrum** (Down) monastic site was enclosed by three concentric stone walls (now partly reconstructed), oddly sited on a glacial island in east Down where earthworks would seem more likely.

27 A third distinctive type of Early Christian settlement site is the *crannog*, a dwelling constructed in a shallow lake, generally the watery equivalent of dry-land raths and cashels. In a few cases crannogs are known to have been royal residences, like the one at Lagore (Meath), but most were occupied by farmers who kept stock and tilled the surrounding land. There is some excavated evidence for prehistoric occupation of crannogs, though doubts remain about whether these were truly crannogs rather than island or lake-shore settlements. There is much excavated evidence to suggest construction from about 500 AD onwards, but some crannogs were used, and perhaps refurbished, as late as the 16th and 17th centuries in times of war. A crannog, perhaps the one in Roughan Lough (Tyr), is shown under attack 26 in one of Richard Bartlett's pictorial maps of about 1600.

A crannog is an artificially constructed 'island', of brushwood, timbers, stakes, stones and rubbish, supporting a platform of wood or stone on which structures of wood or stone were built. It was usually surrounded by a palisade of poles or planks, but in a few cases a stone revetment is found, as at Lough na Cranagh, Fair Head (Ant). Crannogs are more positively

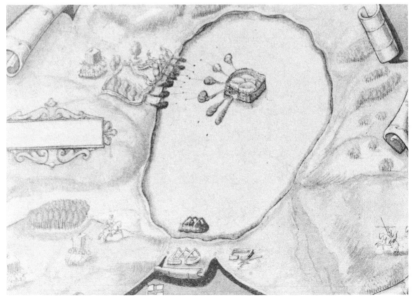

26   *Crannog under attack: detail from Richard Bartlett's map of about 1600.*

defensive than raths or cashels. They are difficult of access, easy to defend in man-to-man combat, and water is a valuable protection against wild animals and fire. Transport seems to have been by dug-out boats, many of which have been found near crannogs.

Crannogs are most commonly found in areas of extensive lakeland, but they tend to occupy small lakes rather than large stretches of water like Lough Erne or Lough Neagh. Examples occur in every county of Northern Ireland but the majority are concentrated in a belt stretching from Fermanagh through south Tyrone and Armagh to mid Down. Occasionally several crannogs occur together, as in Drumgay Lough and Lough Eyes (Ferm). Many crannogs can now be seen as small, tree-covered islands in lakes. There is a prominent example in Lough Brickland (Down), visible from the main road, and others can be seen in Roughan Lough (Tyr), Castle Lough at Stewartstown (Tyr), beside Monea Castle (Ferm), in Ross Lough (Ferm), at Lisleitrim (Arm) and in the lake at Augher (Tyr). Where lakes have been 27 drained a crannog can survive as a hummock, often tree-grown, in a bog or in reclaimed pasture. **Inishrush Crannog** in Green Lough (Ldy), once large and important, is now just visible as a slight rise in the bog. Crannogs are unfortunately somewhat hazardous to visit, whether in bogland or open water, and are best viewed from a distance, as their original builders intended!

27   *Lisleitrim crannog (Arm) with trivallate rath in foreground.*

28   *Knock Dhu Promontory Fort (Ant), air view.*

There is a tendency to regard raths, cashels and crannogs as *the* Early Christian settlement sites, but it is important to recognise other elements in the picture. *Promontory forts* occur on the coast and sometimes inland, where a projecting headland of suitable size, defended naturally by the sea and steep cliffs, was cut off from the mainland by a short stretch of earthworks or walling across the narrow neck of the promontory. In this way a large area could be secured with a minimum of effort. By analogy with British and Continental sites it has been suggested that some of the more spectacular examples, such as Knock Dhu and Lurigethan overlooking the Antrim coast, may have been built in the Iron Age, but excavation at Larrybane on the north Antrim coast produced evidence of Early Christian period activity. Dunseverick (Ant), which appears as an important site in early written sources, can be regarded as an extreme form of promontory fort – almost a stack fort – because of its position on a dramatic sea-girt headland. The rocky headland at **Dunluce** (Ant), with its rock-cut souterrain now within the castle, must also have been an Early Christian period stronghold.

Some settlements of the period are sited on rocky outcrops, difficult of access, suggesting that their builders were anxious to obtain security even at the expense of shelter and convenience. A good example is the Giant's Sconce, south-west of Coleraine (Ldy), where the outcrop was defended by a massive cashel wall, almost completely destroyed in the 19th century. It is

28

similar in its siting to some excavated forts of this period in Scotland. These strongly defensible sites may include some of the royal and aristocratic strongholds known from written sources but difficult to identify from amongst the numerous raths and cashels.

One important royal site was **Tullaghoge Fort** (Tyr), *inauguration place* of the northern Uí Neill. Its superficial appearance is now of a tree-planted hilltop rath, but it is certainly not a 'typical' rath. Within a large outer bank is a wide, flat area, then a considerably raised polygonal inner enclosure. The site was in use from the Early Christian period until 1601, when the Elizabethan general, Mountjoy, destroyed the stone inauguration chair. The fort with its interior buildings, and the stone chair outside, are shown in one of Richard Bartlett's fine pictorial maps made during Mountjoy's campaigns. 132

Recent survey and excavation in Antrim suggests that certain large *upland enclosures*, with house platforms and associated field boundaries, may belong to the Early Christian period. *Unenclosed settlements* of the period are also known. These are by definition difficult to identify since they lack clearly recognisable earthworks or walls, but they are sometimes found from scatters of pottery turned up during ploughing or by the erosion of coastal sand dunes. These seem to have been as popular for settlement, perhaps seasonal, in the Early Christian period as in earlier times. Occasionally the accidental discovery of a souterrain will lead to the identification of an unenclosed house, like the one excavated at Craig Hill (Ant).

29   *Toberdoney Souterrain (Down), partly rock-cut, partly dry-stone.*

30 *Souterrains* have been mentioned in almost every settlement context: in the
23, 24 rath at **Ballywee** (Ant), the cashel at **Drumena** (Down), the promontory
fort at **Dunluce** (Ant) and in open settlements. There are others in ecclesiastical contexts, as at Ballintemple (Ldy), beside Errigal old graveyard. A
souterrain is an artificially built or dug underground structure, popularly
known in the countryside as a 'cave', but not to be confused with natural
caves. Most common is the dry-stone souterrain, made by digging an open
trench, building up dry-stone walls within it, roofing them with large
lintels, and covering the whole with soil. This type is often discovered
accidentally when a lintel is disturbed during ploughing or other work.
Souterrains were also cut or tunnelled into rock or clay, either laterally into a
rock face or in a series of passages, linked by vertical shafts through which
the excavated debris was removed. Sometimes a souterrain shows both
29 structural methods – partly built and partly quarried.

The simplest souterrain plan is of one or two passages or chambers. Frequently, however, there was a sequence of chambers linked by very narrow
'creeps', and sometimes 'blind alleys' were included, or steps or traps of
differing degrees of complexity. Other features include ventilation shafts
and niches or 'cupboards' in the walls. Recent research in Down and Antrim
suggests regional variations in souterrain plans and it seems possible that
there were specialist souterrain builders, as there were specialist builders of
churches and round towers in Early Christian Ireland.

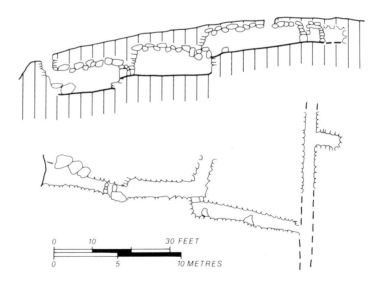

0   10   30 FEET
0   5   10 METRES

30   Dunalis Souterrain (Ldy), section above, plan below.

The function of souterrains has long been a subject for debate and some disagreement. The balance of opinion at present is in favour of their having been refuges, though they could also have been used for storage and perhaps temporary habitation. A few souterrains have ogham-inscribed stones in their fabric, as at Dunalis (Ldy) and Connor (Ant). Finds are rare from excavated examples but the evidence points to the Early Christian period as the time of their building and original use. As in the case of crannogs, a word of warning is needed about visiting souterrains. Except for a few which have been fully secured, like **Drumena** (Down), they are potentially dangerous and should never be entered by a visitor alone, never without local enquiry as to safety and never without waterproof clothing, artificial light and great circumspection.

Ecclesiastical sites and monuments There must have been contacts with Christians in western Britain before 400 AD, but the main conversion of Ireland began in the 5th century and is strongly associated with St Patrick. By the time of the earliest biographical writings about him in the late 7th century his mission was seen as partly in the north, especially in the Lecale area of county Down. The earliest church organisation in Ireland, as in the rest of Christendom, was diocesan, with bishops administering dioceses which probably corresponded to secular kingdoms. The presence of the cathedral church inside the hilltop enclosure at Downpatrick, and the nearness of Clogher cathedral to the great Rathmore earthworks, underline the dependence of early missionaries on royal support. But from the 6th and 7th centuries onwards a monastic organisation developed and monasteries seem to have dominated the Irish church until the reforms of the 12th century. Early Irish monasteries were grouped in 'families', and amongst the most important northern monastic families were those of Columba of Derry and Iona, Comgall of Bangor, Finnian of Movilla, Molaise of Devenish, Eogan of Ardstraw, Cainnech of the Roe Valley area, Monenna of Killevy and, greatest of all, Patrick's centred on Armagh.

Several hundred ecclesiastical sites of the Early Christian period can be pinpointed in Northern Ireland, some still occupied by churches in use, some still used for burial, some preserved as 'monuments', some completely abandoned and neglected, and some lost with no surface traces. We know that there was a wide range in size from large monasteries, centres of considerable population, to small hermitages and retreats, with a poorly-understood range of churches of middling size in between. The large monasteries served many functions in society, maintaining the daily round of services, ministering to lay people, providing education and fosterage for the young, hospitality for travellers, even acting as detention centres for wrong-doers. In some there would be a library and a *scriptorium* for manuscript work, in many workshops for metal, wood and leather crafts, and all would be involved in the agricultural round of arable and stock farming.

31   The northern site where this can best be imagined is **Nendrum** in Strangford Lough (Down), where three concentric stone walls enclose ruined church, round tower stump, graveyard and hut foundations. The plentiful finds from excavation in the 1920s are now in the Ulster Museum. But in general the physical remains of the earliest Christianity, at least to 800 AD, are elusive, for the main building material was wood, and generations of wooden buildings are lost except when they can be recovered by careful excavation. This means that at sites founded in the 6th or 7th centuries the earliest visible remains may not be earlier than the 9th, 10th, 11th or even 12th centuries.

32   One of the earliest Christian monuments is the stone from Drumconwell (Arm), now in Armagh Public Library, carved with a cross and an *ogham inscription*. The ogham alphabet was cumbersome, letters being indicated by groups of strokes on either side of a vertical line, usually the angle of a

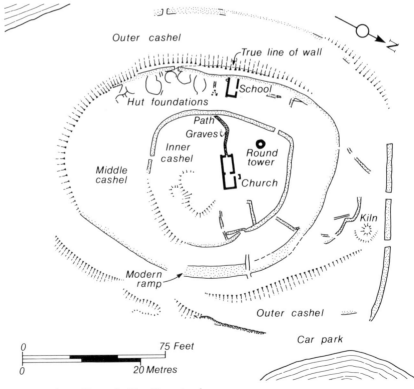

31   Nendrum Monastic Site (Down), plan.

32

32, 33   Ogham Stones: left Drumconwell (Arm); right Aghascrebagh (Tyr).

stone. Ogham inscriptions seem to date especially from the 5th and 6th centuries, and the alphabet was abandoned when an easier form of script was introduced. The main concentration of ogham-inscribed stones is in Munster and they occur only rarely in the north, but an ogham-inscribed pillar stone with no Christian symbols can be seen at Aghascrebagh (Tyr) 33 and another from Topped Mountain is on show in Fermanagh County Museum.

The earliest datable *cross-carved stone* is the tall pillar at **Kilnasaggart** (Arm), 82, 83 dated from its long inscription to about 700 AD. It stands in a cemetery of stone-built graves, which have also been found close to the early churches at **Derry** (Down) and **St John's Point** (Down). Other cross-carved stones can be seen at Killadeas (Ferm), **Maghera** (Ldy), Turraloskin (Ant), Saul (Down) and elsewhere. A common form of grave-marker from the 8th century onwards was the *recumbent cross slab*, sometimes inscribed, seeking a prayer for the dead person. There is a fine example at **Movilla** (Down),

Details of high crosses: Adam and Eve.
34   above left, Arboe (Tyr).
35   above right, Donaghmore (Down).
36   left, Boho (Ferm).

asking for a prayer for Dertrend, and another from Kirkinriola (Ant), now in Ballymena, seeks a prayer for Degen. There is a collection at **Nendrum**, without inscriptions, and in the lower graveyard on **Devenish** (Ferm) a large recumbent slab lies still in position over its grave.

Free-standing *crosses* are probably the best-known feature of early Irish

34

monasteries. Crosses served many purposes, some marking burials but others signifying boundaries or subdivisions of the monastic area. They were focuses for prayer, preaching, penance and perhaps for making oaths. The origins and dating of high crosses are still matters of discussion and dispute, but development in the late 8th century seems likely, as do contacts with similar developments in Northumbria and on Iona. The main period of cross-carving may have been the 9th and 10th centuries.

The northern crosses have suffered from weathering and other damage, and some, like the cross in Armagh cathedral, survive only as battered fragments. The finest of the figure-carved series is at **Arboe** (Tyr), where the 130 two main faces bear scenes from the Old and New Testaments, scenes 34 closely paralleled at nearby **Donaghmore** (Tyr), on the fragment in 131

37 White Island Figure (Ferm):
abbot or bishop, left.

38 Killadeas (Ferm) 'Bishop' Stone, below.

Armagh cathedral, on the broken shaft at Camus (Ldy) and at Clones
35 (Monaghan). In a quite different style the granite cross at Donaghmore
(Down) has some of the same scenes. Early Irish monastic scholarship was
very much scripture-based, and figure-carved crosses could be seen at a
simple level as illustrating scripture, but also as reminders in stone of hymns
and prayers, of the sacraments, of seasons in the church's year, of the
sanctity of Sunday, of the popular David story and of the monastic fathers in
84 the distant Egyptian desert. The cross in **Tynan** village (Arm) combines
figure-carved panels with geometric decoration and circular bosses, whilst
114 the tall cross on **Inishmacsaint** (Ferm) is almost plain. The strange stumpy
II cross in **Errigal Keerogue** graveyard (Tyr) appears to be unfinished,
perhaps because of a flaw still visible in the stone.

There seems to have been a tradition in west Ulster of *figure-carving* in stone.
37 Best-known is the impressive group on **White Island** (Ferm) where the
figures are graded in size and, with sockets in the tops of their heads, seem to
have served some structural purpose. There is no doubt that the figures are
Christian in context, not pagan as has been claimed. They are extremely
powerful pieces of stone carving, not easy to parallel or to date, but a 9th- or
10th-century date is likely. Somewhat similar are the two figure-carved
stones at Carndonagh (Donegal), but closer to hand is the 'bishop' stone at
38 Killadeas (Ferm), with its energetic walking figure with his bell and crozier.

Other kinds of stones found at early ecclesiastical sites include *sundials*, with
three main rays indicating the times of the main daytime services at the
95 third, sixth and ninth hours. Examples can be seen at **Nendrum** (Down),
Bangor (Down) and Clogher (Tyr). Hollowed boulders known as *bullauns*
are quite commonly found in graveyards. They are often thought to be fonts

39   *Ballintemple Bullaun Stone (Ldy).*

I   *Ballymacdermot Court Grave (Arm).*

II   *Errigal Keerogue Cross and Church (Tyr).*

III   Harry Avery's Castle (Tyr).

IV   Dunluce Castle (Ant).

V   Kilclief Castle (Down).

VI   Narrow Water Castle (Down).

VII   Enniskillen Castle: the Watergate (Ferm).

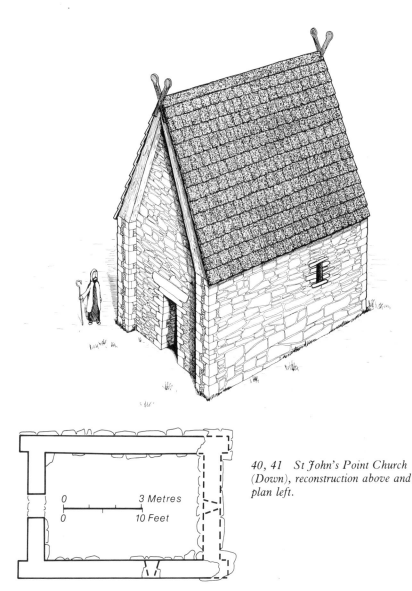

40, 41   *St John's Point Church (Down), reconstruction above and plan left.*

0   3 Metres

0   10 Feet

and some are still used for wart cures, but they were probably originally mortars, used with a pestle or rubbing stone to grind food, animal fodder or other materials (like whin 'knocking-stones' of recent times). The rags on overhanging bushes at **Dungiven** (Ldy) testify to the bullaun's use as a 'wart well'. A bullaun lies beside the holy well at **St John's Point** (Down), and there are others near the **Kilnasaggart** pillar (Arm) and outside Errigal graveyard at **Ballintemple** (Ldy). There is a double bullaun on **Devenish** (Ferm) with hollows back to back and perforated through the bases.

39

40 41
93 Amongst the earliest surviving *churches* in the north are those at **St John's Point** and **Derry** near Portaferry (both Down). They are small simple rectangles with a west door with characteristically sloping jambs, few and small windows, and the features known as *antae*, slight projections of the side walls beyond the gables. The hypothetical reconstruction of St John's Point church shows a roof of wooden shingles, the covering suggested by the steep pitch of the gables, but many churches were probably thatched. At both sites excavation has shown that burials preceded the stone churches and at Derry also an earlier stone and timber building, perhaps an earlier church. A 10th- or 11th- century date is likely for these two small churches. Their small size and simplicity must not blind us to the fact that timber churches, some probably very large and elaborate, were built until the 12th century, and these surviving small stone churches were by no means 'typical'.

At the historically more important sites of **Killevy** (Arm) and **Maghera** (Ldy) the ruined churches are more altered but both incorporate some pre 81 12th-century work, at Killevy notably the massive lintelled west door. On **Inishmacsaint** (Ferm) the west end of the long ruined church is an altered small, pre-Romanesque church of this simple early type. Slightly later is the 51 nave of the fine church at **Banagher** (Ldy). The date 474 was cut on the west door in the 1730s and the nave may, like nearby **Dungiven**, have been built round about 1100-1150.

The earliest written reference to a *round tower* is to one at Slane (Meath) burned by the Vikings of Dublin in 950, and it seems likely that towers were first built in the later 9th or early 10th centuries, their builders influenced by Continental models, known to travelling Irish clerics. Claims of a far earlier, purely Irish, origin do not stand up to critical examination. Round towers served as belfries, for the ringing of hand bells, and also as safe storage places for treasures, books and people. Their raised doors are a defensive feature and the all-stone outer face would help to withstand fire (though some towers *were* burned). Built perhaps first in response to the uncertainties of Viking raids, they continued to be built in the 12th and even 13th centuries. The tower remaining from the once-important monastery at 42 **Antrim** may be 10th or 11th century in date whilst the finely decorated **Devenish** (Ferm) tower is certainly of the 12th century. Surviving stumps 94 include those at **Nendrum** (Down), **Maghera** (Down), Armoy (Ant) and Drumbo (Down).

It is known from written sources that *water mills* were important in Early Christian Ireland, and that there were both 'church mills' and 'lay mills'. An exciting recent discovery has been the identification of several Early Christian mills. Mill stones and structural timbers have been found in drainage

42   Antrim Round Tower.

and sewage excavations, close to small streams. Not only do the remains throw light on economy and technology, but the timbers can be dated precisely by dendrochronology (tree-ring dating). Dates so far range from a 7th-century example in Cork to 8th- and 9th-century mills in Londonderry (Drumard) and Antrim (Rasharkin). Now that the type has been identified, it seems certain that more will be found.

MEDIEVAL MONUMENTS

The 12th century was a period of transition and major change in Ireland in both political and ecclesiastical matters. The political upheavals in the north began in 1177 with the Anglo-Norman invasion of east Ulster led by John de Courcy, a knight from Stogursey in Somerset. The Normans quickly conquered east Antrim and east Down but although these areas were firmly settled the colonisation expanded no further, and from the late 13th century the frontier was gradually pushed back. Eventually Anglo-Norman settlement was restricted to a few coastal enclaves centred on a large castle, like Carrickfergus, or a trading port, like Ardglass.

The Anglo-Norman invasion serves as a valuable archaeological horizon because the newcomers introduced new kinds of equipment and new types of structures. One prominent kind of earthwork, characteristic of the first phase of Anglo-Norman conquest and settlement, was the castle mound –
44, 45 the *motte* or *motte and bailey*. Just as in the case of the Norman conquest of England after 1066, or the later capture of the Welsh border area, the invaders needed strongpoints from which to conquer and control areas of countryside. These took the form of artificially-built flat-topped mounds (mottes), sometimes using a pre-existing rath either as the base of the mound or as a convenient, ready-made annexe (the bailey). It is an attractive hypothesis to suggest that the invaders may have used abandoned raths as ringworks in the very early stages of the conquest, later adding mounds in some cases. A series of mottes, probably used between 1177 and 1220, extends across county Down from Crown Mound near Newry to **Holywood** on Belfast Lough and east to the Ards peninsula. Included in this string of
98, 43 mottes is the great mound at **Downpatrick, Dromore** motte and bailey, **Duneight**, using a pre-Norman enclosure for its bailey, and **Shandon Park Mound** in Belfast. They were sited to secure lines of communication, especially valley routes, and to provide centres for the administration of conquered areas. From field survey, excavation and documentary research we know of about 40 probable mottes in Down and nearly 70 in Antrim.

Typically a motte is a conical flat-topped mound, some 5 metres high and 20

43   Dromore Motte and Bailey (Down), air view (Aerofilms Ltd).

to 25 metres in diameter across the summit, encircled by a ditch, though bigger and smaller examples do occur. It can sometimes be difficult to distinguish an Early Christian raised rath from a low motte from superficial appearance alone, without excavation. Motte excavations in Britain have discovered various kinds of wooden and stone structures on and in the mounds, including timber palisades round the edge of the summit and tall towers on posts in the centre. Excavation at **Clough** (Down) revealed the post-holes of a palisade and pits for archers, but a domestic building rather than a tower in the centre. Domestic buildings have also been found on excavated mottes at Lismahon and Rathmullan in Lecale (Down).   44

Some mottes had attached baileys, earthwork enclosures at a lower level, probably to provide extra accommodation for men, horses, and stores, but the few excavations done in Ulster baileys have not so far been very productive. Baileys are often kidney-shaped with the motte at one side, like **Clough**. This shape is sometimes the result of building a motte in a pre-existing rath, as at Knockaholet (Ant). The best-preserved motte and bailey (in this case rectangular) is in a bend of the Lagan at **Dromore** (Down) and another impressive example is **Harryville** at Ballymena (Ant). Access from bailey to motte was sometimes by a moveable bridge. When this was raised the mound became an isolated stronghold.   45   43

Although some mottes were clearly occupied well into the 13th century (a

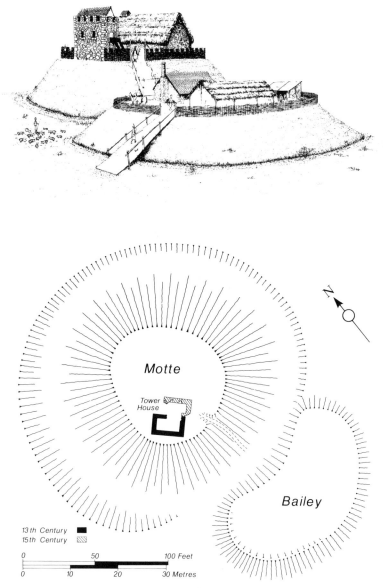

44, 45 *Clough Castle (Down), reconstruction and plan.*

small stone tower was built on **Clough** motte in the 13th century) it is unlikely that motte-building continued much into that century. The summit of a motte was exposed to the weather and severely restricted in area, and once a region was secure it is likely that the mound was abandoned in favour of more comfortable and spacious accommodation. This would perhaps have been supplied by stone castles and by less defensive halls and farms, about which we still know very little.

Stone castles call for a far greater investment of time, money and manpower than earth and timber fortifications and were built mainly for the Crown or by great magnates. Stone castles were built from the earliest years of the conquest, but these were exceptional strongpoints at strategically important places, at a time when most fortifications were of earth and timber. **Carrick-** 46
fergus Castle, on its rocky outcrop dominating Belfast Lough, was started soon after 1177 as one of John de Courcy's chief strongholds. Its earliest phase, started perhaps in 1178, is the polygonal inner ward and the great rectangular keep. At **Dundrum**, dominating Dundrum Bay, the site of a 99 pre-Norman enclosure was chosen for the building of a polygonal curtain wall, the upper ward. The rectangular keep at Carrickfergus was perhaps a little old-fashioned for the late 12th century but the circular keep added at VIII Dundrum in the late 12th or early 13th century was very much up to date, similar to circular keeps in south Wales and the Welsh border, from where many of the invaders came.

The 13th century saw the strengthening of the castles at Carrickfergus (middle and outer wards with the great gatehouse) and Dundrum (a new gatehouse), and the building of some new stone castles. At **Greencastle** (Down) the motte nearer the shore seems to have been abandoned in the

46   *Carrickfergus Castle (Ant) across the harbour.*

43

X   13th century for the stone castle on its rock: a rectangular tower with a large
hall at first floor level, surrounded by a curtain wall with D-shaped angle
towers. Defensive details revealed by excavation at Greencastle include
foundations of a forebuilding protecting the first floor entrance to the hall
and a substantial rock-cut ditch. The gatehouse area is obscured by farm
buildings, but clearly in the 13th and 14th centuries strong gatehouses were
greatly valued to protect the most vulnerable point of a castle. Greencastle in
Inishowen (Donegal) has a fine early 14th-century gatehouse, similar to
some of Edward I's Welsh castles.

Very little is known of the buildings, domestic or defensive, of the Irish
during the medieval period. They were probably mainly of perishable
materials – wood, wattle, clay, turf – and little seems to have survived above
ground. One important masonry building does, however, survive deep in

III Gaelic west Ulster: **Harry Avery's Castle**, near Newtownstewart (Tyr). In
form it is allied to the great gatehouses at Greencastle (Donegal) and Carrickfergus, but in practice the twin-towered 'gatehouse' serves as a keep or
tower. Access to the walled, elevated bailey behind was only by a flight of
steps and a door at first floor level. Unfortunately the castle is difficult to
date. The traditional association with Henry Aimbreidh O'Neill would
suggest a late 14th-century date, but the 15th century is also possible.

Stone castles continued to be important as military and administrative
centres in the later Middle Ages, but few major masonry castles are known
to have been newly built in the 14th and 15th centuries. The English colony
suffered during the Bruce wars from 1312 to 1316, and the 14th century was
a bleak period in Ireland as in Britain, with plague in mid century. But with
the economic recovery of the 15th century came a period of renewed
building activity in a rather different direction, one which involved equally
the Gaelic and Anglo-Norman areas. During the 15th and 16th centuries
hundreds of small stone *tower-houses* were built widely over Ireland. The
densest concentration is in Limerick, Cork and Tipperary, and numbers in
the north are small by Munster standards, but there is an interesting group
in Down and Antrim, in areas settled by Anglo-Norman families. Evidence
for tower-houses in Gaelic areas further west is scarce, though the heads of
important families clearly did build stone towers, for example the Maguires
at **Enniskillen** (Ferm) and the O'Neills at Dungannon (Tyr).

In 1429 Henry VI, in an attempt to settle the country, offered a subsidy of
ten pounds to every liege man of the king in Dublin, Meath, Kildare and
Louth who built a castle within ten years of the proclamation. This sum
cannot have been more than help towards the overall cost: 140 years later, in
the 1570s, **Mahee Castle** cost £300 and **Narrow Water** £361 4s 2d, and even
allowing for inflation it seems likely that a tower-house in the 1430s cost

£100 or more. More significant than the sum offered was the recommended minimum size, 20 by 16 feet in plan and 40 feet or more in height, a size to which most of the northern examples conform.

Though the 1429 subsidy did not apply to the northern counties, the earliest tower-houses in Down may date from quite soon after it. The earliest probably datable example is **Kilclief**, near the coast of Lecale, a residence of   v
John Sely who was Bishop of Down from 1429 to 1443 (when he was ejected for living with Lettice Thomas, a married woman, in his castle of Kilclief). The tall castle has four floors, the first vaulted in stone, with two projecting turrets, one containing the spiral stair and the other a series of garderobes (latrines). These projections are joined at roof-level by an arch covering a drop-hole for directing missiles at unwelcome visitors below (a machicolation). This kind of tower-house is sometimes called the 'gatehouse' type, because of its similarity to a castle gatehouse. Also belonging to the early county Down group is **Audley's Castle**, high on a rocky hill commanding   97
the narrow mouth of Strangford Lough. It has remains of its outer enclosure, or bawn. **Jordan's Castle**, Ardglass, is also of the 15th century, the   101
most imposing of a ring of towers built round the harbour to secure the important Anglo-Norman trading port and provide safe storage space for merchandise. The tower-house overlooking the harbour at **Portaferry** has only one projecting tower, with the door protected by a machicolation in the angle between main tower and projection. It was probably built in about 1500.

47   Layd Church (Ant), wicker centering.

45

The next datable group of tower-houses in county Down clusters in the reign of Elizabeth (1558-1603), continuing into the 17th century. Defensive features were improved and changes in the interior ensured greater comfort. The two projecting towers were found to be unnecessary and the doors at

104 **Strangford** and **Narrow Water** were protected by a small machicolation,
VI supplemented at the latter by a murder-hole inside the door. Here and at **Quoile** a straight stair in the wall thickness served instead of the spiral stair of the earlier towers. Some of the later towers were provided with holes for

108 defence by firearms, for example at **Quoile** and **Kirkistown**, latest of the series (1662). At Kirkistown there are remains of a bawn, with two circular flanker towers at the angles, and a length of bawn wall with gun-loops

104 survives at Walshestown Castle. **Strangford Castle** has no stone vault, but many of the later towers did retain this feature, for greater strength and fire-proofing. At Old Castle Ward much of the centering of wicker mats on which the vault was built survives. Impressions of wicker centering are clear

47 in the vaulted tower at **Layd Church** (Ant), and a modern example of wicker centering has been left in place at **Narrow Water** to illustrate this distinc-

103 tively Irish technique. **Sketrick Castle** is usually dated to the 15th century, but some features suggest that it could be later. On its island site it has a secure boat-bay on the ground floor, a feature shared by nearby **Mahee Castle**.

The clustering of tower-houses for mutual protection, so clear at Ardglass, was also a feature of Carrickfergus, another important port. A view of the 1560s shows the main street lined with towers. None survive above ground but foundations have been found by excavation. **Olderfleet Castle** (Ant) is the one survivor, badly ruined, of three castles which overlooked the anchorage at Larne in the late 16th century, and Castle Chichester at Whitehead (Ant) was built in about 1604. One urban tower-house survives inland at Dromore (Down), badly ruined.

It is possible from a visit to tower-houses, especially the roofed examples, to imagine something of the life-style of the inhabitants. Nowhere is this easier

48, 49 than in **Audley's Castle**, where there are fireplaces, window-seats, cup-boards, latrines and drain holes for slops. It was probably much easier to live in comfort in a tower-house than in one of the earlier large stone castles.

Also of Elizabeth's reign, but in a very different tradition, were the *campaign forts* of Lord Mountjoy's northern expeditions from 1601 to 1603. These forts were strategically sited to command important lines of communication and were quickly built in campaign conditions. Little survives from the 1590s war in the Blackwater valley, but from Mountjoy's north-

86 ward advance in 1601 is **Moyry Castle**, overlooking the Moyry Pass in the

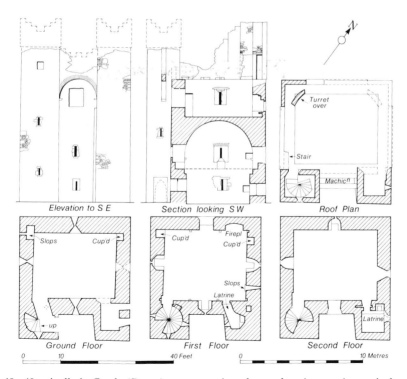

Elevation to S E   Section looking S W   Roof Plan

Turret over

Stair

Machicⁿ

Ground Floor   First Floor   Second Floor

Slops   *Cup'd*

Cup'd   *Firepl*   *Cup'd*

Slops

Latrine

up   *Latrine*

0   10   40 Feet   0   10 Metres

48, 49   *Audley's Castle (Down), reconstruction above; elevation, section and plans below.*

47

mountains of south Armagh. The tall, austere tower, within an outer wall, has rounded corners and layers of musket-loops. The stone and brick blockhouse at **Mountjoy** (Tyr), on the western shore of Lough Neagh, seems to be the castle built by Sir George Carew some time before 1611 to take the place of a larger earthen campaign fort built by Francis Roe during Mountjoy's 1602 advance against O'Neill. It has a square central block with four rectangular corner towers with gun-loops. **Carrickfergus Castle** was altered, probably during the 1560s, for defence by artillery. The curtain walls were pierced by gunports for cannon, distinguished by the use of brick, perhaps the earliest example in Ulster.

The *town* of Carrickfergus was shown enclosed by a simple ditch in the view of the 1560s, but from 1574 onwards the defences were strengthened by a turf bank and later a stone wall, found during excavation in the 1970s. Carrickfergus and Ardglass were not the only urban centres in the late 16th century. The main flowering of Ulster towns belongs to the period of the Plantation, but in the Middle Ages there was clearly some growth of towns, often around an ecclesiastical nucleus. Bartlett's map of Armagh in about 1600 shows a sizeable settlement in ruins. Downpatrick was the site of several religious houses as well as the bishop's seat and must have been a population centre. Newtownards had a court in the Middle Ages in addition to the friary, though it is uncertain how big a settlement Sir James Montgomery found there when he established his town from 1605 onwards. In 1548 a settlement with a market at Newry is mentioned in a document, presumably near the Cistercian Abbey and the castle: a pictorial plan of the 1580s shows a long, narrow town within a rampart, with poorer extra-mural settlement to the north. Other medieval centres of population at ports included Strangford and Coleraine. The extent of at least embryo urban centres in Down and Antrim contributed to the exclusion of these eastern counties from the formal Plantation of Ulster.

Fundamental changes in the early Irish *church* began some decades before the Anglo-Norman invasion. During the late 11th and early 12th centuries certain Irish churchmen were in close contact with Britain and the Continent, and a group of these, leading amongst them the clergy of the Viking towns like Dublin and Waterford, worked to bring Ireland into line with church organisation in the rest of western Christendom. The changes were brought about by a series of synods, from 1101 onwards, which introduced an organisation of fixed dioceses, ruled by bishops, with parishes, tithes and new religious orders. A leading figure in the reforms was St Malachy, a member of a prominent Armagh ecclesiastical family. He encouraged the introduction of the Augustinian Canons, often at early monastic sites like Bangor, Movilla and Saul, and the Cistercians (White Monks), first estab-

*51 Banagher Church
(Ldy), west door.*

49

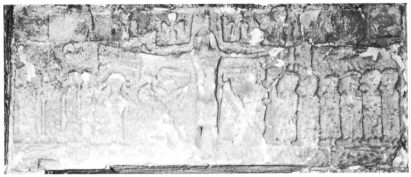

52   Maghera Church (Ldy), lintel of west door.

lished at Mellifont (Louth) in 1142.

Earliest of the 'new' religious houses in the north were SS Peter and Paul at Armagh (1126, Augustinian Canons), Erenagh in Lecale (1127, of the Savignac order) and Newry (about 1153, Cistercian, founded from Mellifont), but no certain trace of these survives above ground. John de Courcy's invasion of 1177 introduced a new direction of monastic influence: his two Cistercian abbeys, Grey and Inch, were founded from mother-houses in northern England, not from Mellifont or Newry. Many of the new episcopal sees were based at early monastic sites, like Ardstraw, Clogher, Down and Dromore, and it seems that the ecclesiastical subdivisions, deaneries, which emerge in medieval written sources were often based on sub-kingdoms of the Early Christian period. More work is needed to understand how this transition worked in detail, but some early churches must have decayed by the early 12th century whilst others survived. As parishes were created they were often based on earlier ecclesiastical units, and parish churches were built at existing church sites. Others were newly sited, close to a lord's chief settlement or motte, or conveniently near to a new centre of population.

Two small stone *crosses* now built into a wall in Downpatrick Cathedral seem to be 12th-century work. They are carved with ecclesiastics with books, similar to, though much smaller than, the 12th-century crosses in Clare, Galway and Tipperary, which seem to emphasise bishops in the context of these 12th-century changes.

Architecturally the 12th century saw a major change, from small simple stone *churches* of pre-Romanesque type at the beginning, to some early Gothic churches, fully in the European architectural mainstream, at the end of the century. From the first half of the 12th century is the nave at
51   **Banagher** (Ldy). Its main feature is the fine west door, superficially 'early' in appearance, with heavy lintel and inclining jambs, but quite sophisti-

cated in treatment. **Dungiven** nave nearby, with an identical window, must be of similar date. **Maghera** (Ldy) west door is structurally of the same type as Banagher but richly decorated with a crucifixion scene on the lintel and Romanesque plant and animal motifs on the jambs. It is possible that this door was inserted into the church at the time of its brief elevation to cathedral status in the mid 12th century. 52

There is sadly little decorated *Romanesque work in situ* in Northern Ireland. The finest is on **Devenish** (Ferm) where St Molaise's 'House' and round tower have decoration of the highest quality, both probably rebuilt after a fire in the 1150s, the 'House' perhaps taking the place of a small, greatly revered wooden church closely associated with the 6th-century founding saint. No trace remains of important documented 12th-century churches at Ardstraw, Bangor and Derry, but decorated Romanesque fragments remind us of lost buildings at Armagh, Devenish, Downpatrick, Inch and Killyleagh.

In marked contrast to the old, haphazardly planned monasteries like **Nen-** 31
drum are the 'new' *monastic foundations*, best represented in county Down at IX
Inch Abbey and **Grey Abbey**, both Cistercian houses, established from 53
Furness (Lancs) in the 1180s and Holm Cultram (Cumbria) in 1193. With them we enter a new world: confidently-handled early Gothic architecture, ambitious in scale, regular in plan, in the Europe-wide Cistercian tradition. In each case the church is north of the cloister, divided in use between the monks to east and lay brothers to west. Graceful grouped lancet windows light the east ends. The cloister was surrounded by a series of rooms for meetings, work, sleeping, eating and storage. The details on the whole are

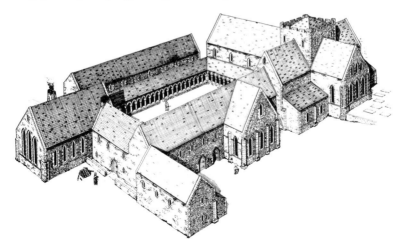

53   *Grey Abbey (Down), reconstruction from the south-east.*

100   simple (except for Grey Abbey's elaborately treated west door), in line with
Bernard of Clairvaux's teaching, and both sites retain the air of seclusion
which the Cistercians sought out and preserved. At Inch much of the
precinct boundary bank and ditch remain, adapted from a pre-Norman
monastic enclosure.

Movilla (Down) was refounded in the late 12th century as an abbey of
Augustinian Canons and its ruined church survives at the edge of the large
graveyard. On the north wall, beside the single pre-Norman grave slab, is a
fine collection of Anglo-Norman grave covers or coffin-lids, trapezoidal
54   slabs carved with 'foliate' crosses, sometimes with a sword or shears to
indicate that a man or woman was commemorated. These 13th-century
coffin-lids are found in the Anglo-Norman-held coastal areas of Down and
Antrim but are particularly concentrated round Newtownards, and this
may have been the centre for their production from the local Scrabo
sandstone. Another early site which continued in use by the Augustinian
Canons was **Dungiven** (Ldy), refounded probably late in the 12th century

52

55   *Dungiven Priory (Ldy), O'Cahan tomb.*

by the O'Cahan family. The 13th-century chancel at Dungiven, once stone-vaulted, is the most accomplished piece of church architecture of its date in mid Ulster, just as the 15th-century tomb against its south wall is the most distinguished late medieval altar tomb in the north. A third early site adapted to Augustinian use was **Killevy** (Arm), occupied by Augustinian nuns. The east church dates from this medieval phase of use. Downpatrick Cathedral incorporates parts of the 13th-century church of the Benedictine Abbey of Down (Black Monks), and the chancel added to the church at **Nendrum** (Down) dates from the foundation of a Benedictine cell there in the late 12th century, but the monastic reoccupation seems to have been short. A fine foliate coffin-lid from the Benedictine Black Abbey in the Ards is now kept at nearby Grey Abbey.

A major event in the late 13th century was the arrival of the friars, mendicant orders vowed to poverty and active in all kinds of work with lay people:

55

56 *Newtownards Friary (Down), 14th-century arcade.*

preaching, teaching and 'social service'. *Friaries* were concentrated espe-
85 cially in and near the main towns. At **Armagh** the fragmentary remains of a
very long 13th-century church survive from the Franciscan (Grey) Friary
founded in 1263-4 on the outskirts of the city. The ruins of the Dominican
(Black) Friary at **Newtownards** (Down) are at the southern approach to the
56 town: a 13th-century nave with a 14th-century arcade and aisle, and 17th-
century additions. Of other friaries known to have existed in Carrickfergus,
Coleraine, Derry, Downpatrick and elsewhere nothing survives above
ground.

It is likely that churches continued to be built of wood beyond the 12th
century, but from the end of that century we can begin to recognise remains
of stone *parish churches*. Two of the earliest and finest were close to Anglo-
Norman castles. St Nicholas's at Carrickfergus, established by John de
Courcy and still in use, has late 12th-century arcades at its west end, and
across the lough at Holywood (Down), not far from the motte, is the ruin of
a late 12th- to early 13th-century parish church, much altered but retaining
very fine cut stonework and details. The substantial ruin in an oval
graveyard at **Maghera** (Down) seems to be 13th century in date. **White
Island** Church (Ferm) with its late Romanesque door was built in about
1200, presumably for parish use, whilst on **Inishmacsaint** (Ferm) the early
church was lengthened eastwards at about the same time, probably for
parish worship. The lower church on **Devenish**, *Teampull Mór*, was built
early in the 13th century as the parish church and not abandoned until the

54

57, 58   Early 13th-century windows at Devenish (Ferm) and Banagher (Ldy).

17th century. Its south window is very similar to the south window of the
added chancel at **Banagher** (Ldy), with elegant multiple roll mouldings.
When the chancel was built in the early 13th century it seems likely that the
founder's grave was disturbed and his remains were deposited in the newly-
built mortuary house, the most accomplished of a small group of these
structures in the north-west. Difficult to date but of the medieval period is
the foundation known as the 'residence' at **Banagher**. It seems to be the only
northern example so far recognised of a strong-house for a clergyman, like
the vicars' pele towers of Northumbria. Ballywillin old church near Portrush
(Ldy) was used until the 19th century; though altered it is substantially of the
early 13th century.

57
58

An important development in Irish religious life in the late Middle Ages
was the establishment of the *Third Order of Franciscan Friars Regular*. This
order made little impact in Britain but flourished greatly in Ireland, especially in strongly Gaelic areas of Ulster and Connacht. The best-preserved
example of their buildings in the north is **Bonamargy Friary** (Ant), traditionally founded by Rory MacQuillan in about 1500. The church windows
retain fine cut stone decoration and the east window had flamboyant (flame-
like) tracery, characteristic of Irish late medieval work and closely paralleled
at Balleeghan (Donegal). St Mary's Augustinian Priory on **Devenish**
(Ferm) may have been founded in the 12th century, but the surviving
remains of church and cloister are of the 15th and early 16th centuries. An
inscription records building work in 1449, but structural and excavated

74

113

59 *Kinawley Church (Ferm), east gable.*

evidence indicate a serious fire later in the century, followed by major repairs and alterations. The church is notable especially for its fine cut stonework, in hard grey limestone. In the graveyard is an unusual, elaborately-decorated cross, also of the 15th century, its head reminiscent of the foliate crosses of coffin-lids.

Some of the patronage which fuelled this late medieval monastic activity also reached the *parish churches*, especially, it seems, in the west. In Fermanagh, for example, Carrick church was founded by Gilbert O'Flanagan and Margaret Maguire in the late 15th century, and other churches of the 15th and early 16th centuries are Templerushin at Holywell, Kinawley, and Derrybrusk church in Fyagh. **Aghalurcher Church** (Ferm) was once substantial and important as chief burial place of the Maguires, but only low foundations of the 15th-century east end remain.

PLANTATION PERIOD AND LATER MONUMENTS

The attempts of Queen Elizabeth I's generals to subdue the Gaelic aristocracy were nowhere more fiercely resisted than in mid and west Ulster by O'Neills, Maguires, O'Donnells and others. James I's advisors took advantage of the Flight of the Earls in 1607 to confiscate land and grant it to people or groups who would undertake to settle and support the king. The English and Scottish planters brought new styles and new craftsmen, and as well as securing their homes were eager to leave their mark as patrons of the church.

Pattern books showing the best of Italian classical design, and English adaptations of those books, were readily available, influencing the design of churches, church monuments and, to a lesser extent, houses. Sir Arthur Chichester's fine monument in St Nicholas's Church at Carrickfergus (1614) was almost certainly carved in Britain and imported, but Sir James Montgomery's at **Grey Abbey** (1652) is a good pattern book example. Hugh, first Viscount Montgomery made sure his initials appeared on the elaborate north door to the tower of **Newtownards Priory** (Down), and another pattern book design nearby is the Market Cross with its shell niches and coats of arms, dated 1636 by inscription.

We have seen that very few medieval churches remain in use, but a number of late 16th- and 17th-century *churches* do survive, roofed and in use. Much of Antrim parish church is of 1596, and St John's on Island Magee (Ant) may be of the 1590s or the very early 17th century. The parish church of Clonfeacle at Benburb (Tyr), built by Sir Richard Wingfield between 1618 and 1622, has a fine Gothic Survival east window. Parts of the old 1622 Donaghmore parish church at Castle Caulfield (Tyr) are built into the 'new church' of 1685 and include another Gothic Survival window, though the 1685 church is thoroughly classical. Donaghadee parish church (Down) was built in 1626 by Hugh, first Viscount Montgomery and retains much of its cruciform design, though the details are changed. Finest of all the Plantation churches is St Columb's Cathedral in Londonderry, which despite many subsequent works remains essentially as built between 1628 and 1633.

Tall bell-towers were added to some existing churches in the 17th century, as at **Maghera** (Ldy), Magheralin (Down) and, with a rebuilt north aisle, at **Newtownards Priory** (Down). All these churches are now ruined, and other ruined 17th-century churches include **Derryloran** at Cookstown, with distinctive intersecting tracery in its east window, Fintona and Bally-clog (all in Tyrone) and Galgorm (Ant). Classical fragments in ruined churches range in style and quality from the simple round-headed door dated 1636 at **Loughinisland** and the door and window dated 1639 at Tullynakill (both Down) to the strikingly studded doorway at Derrygonnelly (Ferm), with the arms of Sir John Dunbar proclaiming the patron who built it in 1627.

60

The English and Scots settlers needed *strong houses and enclosures* in their unfamiliar and potentially hostile surroundings. By the early 17th century

60, 61   Derrygonnelly Church (Ferm), west door left; Old Castle Archdale (Ferm) right.

in England there was no tradition of building defended houses, but the Scottish settlers knew the castles and bawns still being built in their home-lands, ideal for the unsettled conditions in Ulster. The Plantation buildings, erected between 1610 and 1640, consisted of houses, usually fortified and often with an attached walled yard or bawn, and bawns, where the enclosure wall was the main defence, sheltering less substantial structures within.

Not surprisingly English planters tended to introduce English styles. The unusual cross-shaped plan of Sir Anthony Cope's Castleraw (Arm) of about 1620 was derived from his home area in the English midlands. At **Dungiven** and **Brackfield** (both Ldy) Sir Edward Doddington built courtyard houses on the Skinners' Company lands. The houses, shown in early 17th-century drawings to have been in the latest Jacobean style, formed one side of a walled enclosure. Sir William Cole's Portora Castle (Ferm), built in 1618, was of similar plan, as were the London Company founda-tions at Ballykelly and Movanagher (Fishmongers') and Salterstown (Salters'), all in Londonderry. Ruins of a substantial house survive at **Old Castle Archdale** (Ferm), forming one side of a bawn. The bawn gateway is intact, with an inscription recording its building by John Archdale in 1615.

Further east, in the Ards peninsula of county Down, the Savage family adopted two different answers to the problem of security. At **Kirkistown** they built a tower-house, complete with a spiral stair and ogee-headed windows, within a bawn, as late as 1622. Traditionally Irish and thoroughly old-fashioned by this date, it was nevertheless considered a suitable form of

123

61

108

58

secure habitation. A few miles away, near Cloghy, a member of the Savage family built the **White House, Ballyspurge**, perhaps in the 1640s. Originally in a bawn, this was a smaller house with steeply pitched roof and thick walls, pierced by pistol-loops for defence, fully in the 17th-century tradition.

Planters from Scotland brought with them a tradition of defensive building which was still very much alive. In their castles we find distinctive Scottish plan types and details of elevation, like crow-stepped gables and projecting stairs and turrets supported on layers of corbelling. **Monea Castle** (Ferm), built for Malcolm Hamilton from 1618-19, bears a striking resemblance to Claypotts Castle near Dundee, with its corbelled turrets, while Ballygalley Castle (Ant), built in 1625 for James Shaw of Greenock, is easy to parallel in Scotland. Roughan (Tyr) has a more unusual plan, a square central block with substantial circular towers to full height at each corner. Corbelled stair turrets are prominent features at **Castle Balfour** (Ferm) and Aughentaine (Tyr), the latter with twelve courses of corbelling. **Tully Castle** (Ferm), built by Sir John Hume by 1618-19, survives as a substantial ruin, despite its burning and abandonment in 1641. Building for a Scottish planter, Irish craftsmen introduced traditional features like the barrel vault and tapering walls in the T-shaped castle. The so-called watergate at **Enniskillen Castle** (Ferm), which is a waterfront tower, not a gate, has clear Scottish features. Its date has been much debated but 1615 to 1620 seems likely.

Bawns have been mentioned many times in this account and deserve rather

62   Roughan Castle (Tyr).

63 *Ballygalley Castle (Ant)*.

more discussion. The enclosure wall could be strengthened at two, three or four corners by flanker towers, projecting to allow flanking fire along the wall faces. Flankers could be circular or rectangular and the larger towers could provide extra accommodation. This was the case at Bellaghy (Ldy) and **Dalway's Bawn** (Ant), in circular towers. At **Tully Castle** (Ferm), the four rectangular flankers served as small 'houses' with fireplaces and ovens. At Sir Richard Wingfield's bawn, **Benburb Castle** (Tyr), built in about 1615, there seems never to have been a separate house, but the two square flankers had rooms at three levels and must have provided comfortable accommodation. The bawn walls at Benburb are well-supplied with musket-loops for defence, a feature also at Salterstown (Ldy). There are loops in the flanker towers at **Brackfield** (Ldy) and in walls and flankers at **Kirkistown** (Down).

Standing somewhat apart from this fortified tradition is a small group of very *grand houses* which clearly showed the Renaissance tastes and aristocratic pretensions of their builders. The two great houses built by Sir Arthur Chichester, Joymount at Carrickfergus and Belfast Castle, if they had

78
117

133

survived, might have provided a distant echo of Hardwick Hall or Longleat. On a smaller scale the house built in 1620-24 inside Charlemont Fort (Arm) by Sir Toby Caulfield, demolished as recently as 1921, illustrated the same awareness of architectural composition and control. Only two ruins remain to remind us of this type of building. Caulfield's other grand house at **Castle Caulfield** (Tyr) was of half-н plan with generous mullioned windows (considerably altered and strengthened after the trouble of 1641). The great hall house built by Randall MacDonnell, second Earl of Antrim, within the defences at **Dunluce** (Ant) had three tall bay windows and Renaissance detailing of door and fireplace, probably reflecting the tastes of his English wife, the Dowager Duchess of Buckingham.

134

64

Comparatively little is known about the *humbler houses* of the Plantation period, apart from Thomas Raven's valuable pictorial maps of the 1620s. They were built of rubble, mud, turf, timber and thatch and clearly suffered badly in the wars of the 17th century. English timber-framed houses imported into county Londonderry were inappropriate in the wet Irish climate. Much knowledge could be gained from excavation, recently demonstrated in an urban context in Linenhall Street, Londonderry. The lower parts of two 17th-century houses were found with large fireplaces and domed brick ovens. Dendrochronology, tree-ring dating, is also helping in the identification and dating of later 17th-century houses, ranging from grand mansions to modest farm houses. On a larger scale is the old Custom

64   Dunluce Castle (Ant), great hall.

65 *Bangor Custom House (Down).*

65   House at Bangor harbour (Down), built by Lord Clandeboye with government help in 1637. With flanking tower, corbelled turret and crow-stepped
gables it clearly betrays its proprietor's Scottish origins.

Some *traditional buildings*, almost entirely of stone including the roof, are
probably of this period, though they are difficult to date because of the
109   long-lasting, simple techniques of construction. At **Struell Wells** (Down)
the springs and wells are housed in a series of small stone-roofed buildings in
which a pointed barrel vault, a corbelled dome and evidence for wicker
centering are all found. Traditionally frequented by St Patrick, the site was
certainly used in medieval times but the surviving stone structures are
unlikely to be earlier than the 17th century. Corbelled roofs were used for
small farm buildings like pig crews and well covers as late as the 19th
century. Corbelling was also used to roof sweat houses, though the one
example in State Care at **Tirkane** (Ldy) is lintelled. This method of com-
munal cleansing is documented from the 18th and 19th centuries, but its
origins may go back much further. The Tirkane house is built into the valley
side and covered with turf.

Town defences were provided at a number of places in the early 17th century, both in east Ulster and in the planted counties. Belfast had an enclosing bank and ditch, while Sir Arthur Chichester completed the long defensive sequence at **Carrickfergus** with a stone wall (1611-15). Large stretches are easily visible to north and east, as well as North Gate and the excavated wall and Irish Gate foundations in Delaney Green. Coleraine had earthen banks and ditches with a gridded street pattern within, but the ramparts have disappeared. At **Londonderry** Sir Edward Doddington's stone walls were completed in 1618 and these remain largely intact, Ulster's finest urban defences. A wide earthen rampart was faced with stone walls some 7 metres high, protected by eight bastions and four gates. None of the original gates survive (the earliest is Bishop's Gate of 1789) but five of the bastions do, and it is still possible to walk the whole circuit of the wall top.

124
125

Artillery forts in the Europe-wide tradition of thick earthen ramparts with projecting spear-shaped bastions were built in Ireland all through the 17th century. At Charlemont (Arm) the fort was completed by 1624 and added to in 1673. In its final form it was a concentric, star-shaped composition, with massive outer banks and a stone-faced inner enclosure. The gatehouse and earthworks survive. In the mid 17th century **Hillsborough Fort** (Down) was built by Colonel Arthur Hill (on the site of an Early Christian period rath) to command the main route from Dublin to Carrickfergus and Belfast. The square earthwork is stone-faced with spear-shaped angle bastions. The original gatehouse was remodelled in 1758 to form the gothick

66
106

XI

66   *Hillsborough Fort (Down), interior with Early Christian rath ditch exposed.*

67   Moy Gates and Screen (Tyr), detail.

'castle' which now dominates the south-east rampart. Similar artillery forts were built in the late 17th century, including Fort Hill, Enniskillen (Ferm), now lacking its stone face, built in 1689, and Fortwilliam in Belfast, perhaps of similar date. From 1804 to 1812 the coasts of Britain and Ireland were defended against the very real threat of Napoleonic invasion by a series of Martello Towers. The only example in Northern Ireland at **Magilligan** (Ldy), facing another at Greencastle in Donegal, was built in 1812 to a standard pattern. Its first floor entrance, protected by a corbelled machicolation, links it with the medieval castle tradition, though its fire-power (a swivelling 24-pounder gun) was far superior to any earlier method of defence. The round gatehouse towers of **Carrickfergus Castle** (Ant), already lowered for use as gun platforms in the 16th century, were altered again to carry heavier cannon. The castle's collection includes fine examples of late Georgian and mid Victorian cannon.

Few structures of the 18th and 19th centuries have been taken into State Care. Since 1972 historic buildings legislation has provided a special form of protection (listing and grant aid) for buildings still capable of modern use. 107 **Hillsborough Market House**, extended to its present form by about 1810 and still in use as a court house, was taken into care in 1957, before such protection was available. Two particularly fine examples of *ironwork* are in State Care. The wrought iron screen and gates from **Richhill** (Arm), made in 1745, were repaired and moved in 1936 to Hillsborough Castle, facing the Market House. Far heavier but equally fine of their type are the cast iron screen and gates at **Moy** (Tyr), formerly of Roxborough Castle, made in the mid 19th century.

111

67, 68

Ballycopeland Windmill (Down) is a late 18th-century tower mill, disused since the 1914-18 war, but recently restored to working order. *Industrial monuments* of the last two centuries are a subject of growing concern since machinery needs constant care and regular use if it is to survive, yet obsolete machinery has no place in the modern world of commerce and industry. Apart from Ballycopeland Windmill very few industrial monuments are open for public inspection, but the Ulster Folk and Transport Museum at Cultra (Down) has moved water-driven scutch and spade mills to the museum as well as a wide range of farm and other buildings. Wellbrook beetling mill (Tyr) has been preserved and presented *in situ* by the National Trust.

105

The *repair and maintenance* of historic monuments in State Care are carried out by a specialist work force that is in itself worthy of note. Its masons, joiners and smiths keep alive and sometimes revive skills which are in danger of being lost as 20th-century technology has moved towards concrete and steel. But at the same time they must understand and employ sophisticated engineering techniques to underpin, prop or tie the fragments of megaliths, ruined churches, castles and other monuments which are the subject of this guide.

69, 70

1

68   *Moy Gates and Screen (Tyr).*

69   *Tully Castle (Ferm) before conservation from the south-west.*

70   *Tully Castle during conservation from the south-east.*

Inventory

County Antrim

PREHISTORIC MONUMENTS

1 Ballylumford Dolmen (D431016)

71

Close to the NW tip of Island Magee, reached by the B90 road, or by foot passenger ferry from Larne. Now somewhat unexpectedly in the front garden of a house and popularly known as the Druid's Altar, this may be a portal grave, a Neolithic burial monument now denuded of its cairn, or the remains of a passage grave.

PSAMNI (1940), 35.

71   Ballylumford Dolmen.

2 Craigs: The Broad Stone (C979175)

3 miles (4·8 km) N of Rasharkin, on the W side of Long Mountain, approached from the NW through rough, boggy upland (a long walk). A shallow forecourt leads to three chambers in a long, stone-revetted cairn. Despite the superficial appearance of a 'dolmen', created by propping a large capstone on the portals in recent times, this is a well-preserved court grave. ⅓ mile SW is Craigs Dolmen, seven uprights supporting a capstone,

69

perhaps the burial chamber of a passage grave.

PSAMNI (1940), 22.

4 **3 Dooey's Cairn** (D021182)
¾ mile (1·2 km) SSE of Dunloy in Ballymacaldrack townland, reached by a side road W off the B93. Court grave excavated in 1935 and 1975, dated from charcoal to between 3000 and 2500 bc. U-shaped forecourt leads to a stone chamber with, beyond, a long 'cremation passage' with three circular pits. The cairn's edges are revetted with stone.

72

E E Evans in *Ulster J Archaeol* 1 (1938), 59-68; A E P Collins in *Ulster J Archaeol* 39 (1976), 1-7.

72   *Dooey's Cairn, court during excavation in 1975.*

4 Duncarbit Standing Stones (D147347)
⅓ mile (0·5 km) SE of Killuca Bridge, reached by a long, rough, undefined route. Two tall, slender standing stones may be the remains of a once more extensive stone alignment. Local name 'Slaght' suggests burial traditions.

73 **5 Ossian's Grave (or Cloghbrack)** (D213284)
In Lubitavish townland, 1¾ miles (2·8 km) WNW of Cushendall, reached by a track S off the Cushendall-Ballymoney road. Uphill walk from carpark at foot of hill. Hillside court grave with fine views to Glendun, Glenaan and Scotland. Semicircular forecourt opens into a two-chambered burial gallery, formerly set in a short oval cairn. Romantically named after the Early Christian warrior-poet but built in Neolithic times.

PSAMNI (1940), 19.

73 Ossian's Grave.

EARLY CHRISTIAN PERIOD MONUMENTS

6 Antrim Round Tower (J154878)   42
N of the town in Steeple townland, in the grounds of Antrim Borough
Council offices. Though the tower now stands among lawns and trees it was
once surrounded by monastic buildings. Antrim was an important early
monastery, probably a 6th-century foundation, closely linked with Bangor.
The round tower is some 28 m high with the usual raised door but,
unusually, a cross-carved stone above the lintel. There are eight simple,
flat-headed windows. Not closely datable but a 10th- or 11th-century date
seems likely. Interior not accessible. The 'Witch's Stone' nearby contains
two hollows and is a form of bullaun stone.

Ordnance Survey Memoir for the Parish of Antrim (Public Record Office of
Northern Ireland, 1969), 74-8; Gwynn and Hadcock 1970, 28.

7 Ballywee Rath and Souterrains (J218899)
4½ miles (7·2 km) ENE of Antrim, E of the minor road between Parkgate
and Connor. Complex rath with souterrains, excavated in 1974 and now   23
preserved. See pages 23–4 for plan and details. Only earthworks now visible.

Publication by C J Lynn in a future volume of *Ulster J Archaeol*.

8 Coshkib Rath Pair: The Twin Towers (D234292)
1 mile (1·6 km) N of Cushendall, beautifully sited at over 500 feet, overlook-

ing sea and glens. Two circular embanked enclosures close together, one with a waterlogged interior. These may not be 'ordinary' Early Christian farmstead enclosures but their nature is uncertain without excavation.

9   Lissue Rath (J228633)
N of the A3 road between Lisburn and Moira, reached from the northward minor road at Englishtown. Excavation by the late Professor Gerhart Bersu in 1946-7 showed that the circular banked and ditched enclosure, superficially unimpressive, was a complex Early Christian farmstead with a huge structure of concentric post rings filling the centre.

G Bersu in *Ulster J Archaeol* 11 (1948), 131-3; full (posthumous) report to be published in monograph form by HMSO.

10   Spring Farm Rath (J149882)
1 mile (1·6 km) N of Antrim, S of Stiles Way. A well-preserved platform rath, sited on fairly level ground rising gently to the NE. The platform, 30 m in diameter, is surrounded by a ditch 1 m deep but originally much deeper. This was the homestead of a farming family in the Early Christian period but traces of their house and farm buildings could only be recovered by excavation. The rath is now an attractive landmark with mature trees on the platform and varied plant and bird life.

MEDIEVAL MONUMENTS

74   ## 11   Bonamargy Friary (D126408)
½ mile (0·8 km) E of Ballycastle, S of the A2 to Cushendun in Ballycastle golf course. A Third Order Franciscan Friary, traditionally founded by

74   Bonamargy Friary from the north-east.

Rory MacQuillan in about 1500 and used until the mid 17th century. The approach is through a gatehouse set in an earth bank. The long narrow church has three windows and a door in the s wall and a two-phase E window with broken flamboyant tracery. N of the church was a cloister and in the E range is the sacristy for storing equipment, a day-room for indoor work and the friars' dormitory above. The 17th-century vault running s from the church is the burial place of the MacDonnells, Earls of Antrim.

F J Bigger and W J Fennell in *Ulster J Archaeol* special volume (1898); Gwynn and Hadcock 1970, 269; DOENI guide-card (1977).

12   Carrickfergus Castle (J415873)   46

At the w approach to Carrickfergus on the coast road (A2) from Belfast. Large carpark nearby. Strategically sited on a rocky promontory to command Belfast Lough. Begun by John de Courcy soon after his 1177 invasion of Ulster, the castle played an important military role until 1928. Its long history includes sieges by King John in 1210 and Edward Bruce in 1315, the arrival of William III in 1690, and capture by the French under Thurot in 1760. In the 1939-45 war the castle was used for air-raid shelters.

Earliest is the polygonal inner ward on the tip of the rock, begun in about 1178, built in one programme with the great keep. The middle ward was added between 1217 and 1222 with a postern gate to the sea and the east tower with its cross-bow loops. The outer ward and gatehouse were probably built between 1226 and 1242, taking in the full extent of the rocky promontory. Later changes were mainly concerned with firearms provision and the castle's use as an ordnance depot. Cannon from the 16th to 19th centuries are on show and the keep houses a historical display.

Guide book (HMSO, 1962); DOENI guide-card (1977); T E McNeill, *Carrickfergus Castle* (1981), HMSO monograph.

13   Cranfield Church (J055853)   75

On the shore of Lough Neagh at Churchtown Point, 3¾ miles (6 km) SW of Randalstown. Large carpark at lough shore. This small ruined church in its graveyard was the medieval parish church, probably abandoned in the 17th century. The ruin is simple and difficult to date but may be 13th century. A wooden cross inside is a replica of an ancient timber *termon* cross, formerly N of the church, marking the boundary of church lands. Nearby on the shore to the E is a famous holy well, until the 19th century much visited in May and June.

PSAMNI (1940), 42.

75   *Cranfield Church on the shore of Lough Neagh.*

IV **14 Dunluce Castle** (C904414)

Spectacularly sited beside the coast road (A2) between Portrush and Bushmills. Carpark at entrance. The *dún* name and rock-cut souterrain suggest Early Christian period occupation on the rocky headland. The earliest parts of the castle are probably 14th century but it is not documented until the 16th, when it was in the hands of MacQuillans and later MacDonnells. Badly damaged in an artillery attack by the English Deputy, Sir John Perrott, in 1584, the castle was repaired and extended by Sorley Boy and James MacDonnell, but decayed from the later 17th century onwards.

The rectangular mainland court with 17th-century domestic and service buildings leads downhill to the 'funnel', converging walls to channel people or stock towards the gap, now crossed by a fixed wooden bridge but formerly by a drawbridge. The gatehouse with its corbelled-out turrets is of about 1600 and is Scottish in style. Apart from the circular NE and SE towers and parts of the curtain walls, most of the buildings on the rock date from the 16th and early 17th centuries. Close to the S curtain wall a row of column bases is the remains of an Italian-style *loggia* or covered way, based probably on a Scottish model. Dominating the yard is the two-storey hall range with

64   its ruined bay windows, built in the early 17th century. Beyond were service rooms, a kitchen and a lower yard with domestic ranges. Much original paving and cobbling survives in the castle.

Guide book (HMSO, 1966); DOENI guide-card (1977).

15 Harryville Motte and Bailey (D112026)

Prominently sited on the N bank of the river Braid on the S outskirts of Ballymena in Ballykeel townland. Substantial earthwork castle, presumably of the Anglo-Norman invasion period, one of a group in the Ballymena area. Large motte to W and rectangular bailey to E.

PSAMNI (1940), 30.

16 Kinbane Castle (D088439)

In Cregganboy townland, 2½ miles (4 km) NW of Ballycastle, reached by a side turning N off the B15. From a large cliff-top carpark a steep path leads to the shore, across treacherous rocks and up to the castle. This is set on the *ceann bán*, the white (chalk) headland, in a position of great natural strength. Built by Colla Dubh MacDonnell in 1547, it was captured and partly destroyed by the English in 1551, but was reoccupied. The tall remaining fragment is of a three-storey tower beside the gate. Beyond are traces, largely grass-grown, of a walled enclosure.

PLEASE NOTE: this site is dangerous because of eroding rock and steep drops. Great care is needed.

PSAMNI (1940), 6.

76 Kinbane Castle.

17 Layd Church (D245289)

In Moneyvart townland, 1 mile (1·6 km) NE of Cushendall, approached by a

77   *Layd Church from the south.*

footpath off the coast road to Torr Head. The ruined church in its graveyard stands beside a fast-flowing stream above the sea at Port Obe. Though traditionally a Franciscan foundation, this was a parish church in 1306 and continued in use until 1790. The fabric shows at least four phases of medieval and post-medieval remodelling. The long narrow church had a tower at the w end, perhaps providing residential accommodation for the priest. Marks of wicker centering are clear under its vault. Fine gravestones in the yard include MacDonnell memorials and illustrate the area's maritime and Scottish connections.

47

F J Bigger and W J Fennell in *Ulster J Archaeol* 5 (1898), 35-46; *PSAMNI* (1940), 17-18.

18   Muckamore Priory (J167854)

1½ miles (2·4 km) SE of Antrim. The *site* of this priory of Augustinian Canons is in State Care awaiting further excavation to supplement work done in 1973 and eventual display. No standing remains above ground.

Gwynn and Hadcock 1970, 188-9; C J Lynn, excavation report in a future volume of *Ulster J Archaeol*.

19   Olderfleet Castle (D413016)

On the shore of Larne harbour on the tongue of land called the Curran. John Speed's 1610 map of Larne shows three castles around the harbour, *Coraine, Tchevet* and *Olderfleete*. Despite its modern name this ruin is clearly *Coraine*; the other two have disappeared. The square, four-storey tower, badly ruined on the s, has pairs of gun-loops in the basement and may have been a defended warehouse as well as controlling access to the harbour. There are no closely datable features but a 16th-century date is likely.

PSAMNI (1940), 33; E M Jope in *Ulster J Archaeol* 23 (1960), 100.

PLANTATION PERIOD MONUMENTS

20 Carrickfergus Town Walls (J415876 and area)
Lord Deputy Sir Arthur Chichester enclosed Carrickfergus with stone walls from 1611 onwards, and at least half of this circuit is still visible, often to its full height of 4 m to the wall-walk. The wall extended from the castle NW to Irish Gate, then N to North Gate, E to the rear of the Joymount property and S towards the water. The best-preserved stretch of wall with the NE corner bastion can be seen in Shaftesbury Park next to the bowling green. Other features include North Gate at the end of North Street, twice restored in the 20th century but with some 17th-century stones still visible in the arch, and at the end of West Street the footings of Irish Gate and the adjacent wall. This was excavated from 1977 to 1979 by the late T G Delaney, after whom the park, Delaney Green, is named.

PSAMNI (1940), 49; report on the excavations forthcoming by M L Simpson as HMSO monograph.

21 Dalway's Bawn (J443914) 78
3 miles (4·8 km) NE of Carrickfergus on the W side of the B90 road to Ballycarry in Ballyhill townland. An unusually well-preserved example of an early 17th-century planter's fortified enclosure, built in about 1609 by John Dalway to secure his royal grant of land in the area. Now enmeshed with a working farm, only part of the bawn is in State Care – the roadside wall and three flanker towers. A dwelling house formerly inside the bawn has disappeared.

A T Lee in *Ulster J Archaeol* 6 (1858), 125-132; *PSAMNI* (1940), 40.

78 *Dalway's Bawn.*

County Armagh

PREHISTORIC MONUMENTS

4   **22   Annaghmare Cairn** (H905178)
1¾ miles (2·8 km) N of Crossmaglen in rough, boggy country. Park near the
road and approach on foot through the forestry plantation. Court grave,
known locally as the Black Castle, and one of the finest examples in the
2   north. The trapezoidal cairn encloses a three-chambered burial gallery,
3   approached from the S through a horseshoe-shaped forecourt. The fine
dry-stone walling is especially clear in the court. Excavation in 1962-3
showed that the cairn had been extended northwards and two further
chambers added, approached from the cairn's long sides. The rough N end
suggests that a further extension was planned but never accomplished.
Burned and unburned bone, flints and Neolithic pottery were found during
the excavation.

D M Waterman in *Ulster J Archaeol* 28 (1965), 3-46.

5   **23   Ballykeel Dolmen and Cairn** (H995213)
4½ miles (7·2 km) SW of Camlough at the W foot of Slieve Gullion. Portal (or
tripod) dolmen stands at the S end of a long cairn, now 0·6 to 0·9 m high,
with a stone cist (not now visible) near the N end. The dolmen is formed of
two tall portal stones, with a high sill between, and a lower backstone,
supporting a huge capstone, reinstated from a slipped position after excavation in 1963. Bone did not survive but there were plentiful finds of Neolithic
pottery.

A E P Collins in *Ulster J Archaeol* 28 (1965), 47-70.

4   **24   Ballymacdermot Cairn** (J066240)
2 miles (3·2 km) SW of Newry on the road to Killevy Churches near Bernish
viewpoint. Court grave set on the S slopes of Ballymacdermot Mountain,
with extensive views over the Meigh plain to Slieve Gullion and the ring
dyke mountains. The long, trapezoidal cairn had an almost enclosed circu-
1   lar forecourt at its N end, leading to an ante-chamber and two burial
chambers. Parts of the corbelled roofs of these chambers still survive. First
excavated in the early 19th century, the cairn was investigated in 1962 when
Neolithic pottery and flints were found.

A E P Collins and B C S Wilson in *Ulster J Archaeol* 27 (1964), 3-22.

78

25 Clonlum North Cairn (J045213)

4 miles (6·4 km) sw of Newry, E of the foot of Slieve Gullion. The remains of a court grave, badly damaged in the early 19th century when stone was removed for building Killevy Castle nearby. The court is of three-quarter enclosed form with an unusual small chamber in the W horn. The burial gallery lacks subdividing stones but its length suggests originally 3 or 4 chambers. Not excavated.

J Bell in *Newry Magazine* 2 (1816), 235; *PSAMNI* (1940), 78.

26 Clonlum South Cairn (J046206)

4 ½ miles (7·2 km) sw of Newry, ⅓ mile (0·5 km) E of Killevy Castle, in a field on the E side of a minor road. A roughly circular cairn, partly encroached on by cultivation, encloses a single rectangular chamber built of large slabs with a huge, now broken, capstone. Excavation in 1934 showed that the site was already thoroughly disturbed and produced few finds.

O Davies and E E Evans in *Co Louth Archaeol J* 8 (1934), 164-8.

27 Clontygora Cairn (J098194) 79

4 miles (6·4 km) s of Newry within the SE area of the ring dyke, approached from a by-road E off the A1. A court grave, locally known as the King's Ring, excavated in 1937, badly damaged but still impressive. The U-shaped forecourt led into a burial gallery of probably three chambers. Court and chambers are built of very large stones with some roofing slabs still in position, but little cairn material survives. Finds from the excavation included cremated bone, flints and Neolithic pottery.

O Davies and T G F Paterson in *Proc Belfast Nat Hist Phil Soc* 1 part 2 (1938), 20-42.

79 Clontygora Cairn.

80 **28 Navan Fort** (H847452 and area)
2 miles (3·2 km) w of Armagh, reached from a by-road N of the A28 to
Killylea. Carpark at entrance. Site identified as *Eamhain Macha*, chief
residence of the Kings of Ulster and prominent in heroic literature and
legend, traditionally destroyed in 332 AD. A huge, almost circular enclosure
of over 12 acres occupies the summit of a low but commanding glacial hill.
Its ditch is *inside* the bank and the enclosure is most impressive on its s and w
sides. In the NW part of the interior is a tall mound, reconstituted after
excavation in the 1960s and early 1970s. The earliest finds were Neolithic.
From the mid first millennium BC was a series of circular houses with
attached 'yards', all timber-built and representing many generations of use.
19 These were replaced by a massive structure, 40 m in diameter, built of
concentric rings of large posts round a central post. This structure was later
filled with stones and burned, and a mound of sods and clay built over the
18 basal stone cairn to an overall height of about 5 m. Occupation on this site
had certainly ended by about 100 BC, in the Iron Age. A low circular
enclosure near the centre of the fort was also excavated, but no work was
done on the enclosing earthworks. Limestone quarrying has approached
very close to the E side of the fort and has largely obliterated Loughnashade,
find-spot of the famous decorated Iron Age trumpet.

Current Archaeology 22 (1970), 304-8; full report by D M Waterman will
appear (posthumously) in an HMSO monograph.

80   Navan Fort, air view from the east.

7, 8 **29 Slieve Gullion South Cairn** (J025203)
On the s summit of Slieve Gullion, approached from the s by a forest road,

80

followed by a steep, rough climb, or from the N by a long, rough path. At 1894 feet this is the highest surviving passage grave in the British Isles. Access is difficult but the views are spectacular. A circular cairn with a revetment of large stones encloses an octagonal chamber reached along a short passage. The passage is roofed with lintels, the chamber with corbelled stones, now partly collapsed. Excavation in 1961 showed that the burial deposits were badly disturbed, but there were fragments of cremated bone and flints. The 'bulge' on the cairn's N side results from the addition of a small round cairn, perhaps in the Bronze Age, but excavation produced no finds.

A E P Collins and B C S Wilson in *Ulster J Archaeol* 26 (1963), 19-40; A G Smith and J R Pilcher in *Ulster J Archaeol* 35 (1972), 17-21.

30 Slieve Gullion North Cairn (J021211)   13
At the N end of Slieve Gullion summit ridge, at about 1750 feet, approached by the same routes as the South Cairn. A round cairn without kerb stones. Excavation in 1961 revealed two small cists, one with fragments of food vessel pottery and burned bone, suggesting an earlier Bronze Age date.

References as for South Cairn.

EARLY CHRISTIAN PERIOD MONUMENTS

31 Killevy Churches (J040220)
3 miles (4·8 km) s of Camlough and 3½ miles (5·6 km) sw of Newry, on the

81 Killevy Churches, west door of west church.

81

lower E slopes of Slieve Gullion in Ballintemple townland. This is the site of one of Ireland's most important early nunneries, founded by St Monenna (Darerca or Bline) in the mid or late 5th century. It was plundered by Vikings from Strangford Lough in 923. Monastic life continued in the Middle Ages: Killevy was a convent of Augustinian nuns until its suppression in 1542. A large granite slab in the N part of the graveyard traditionally marks St Monenna's burial. A round tower near the SW corner of the church is known to have fallen in the 18th century and no trace survives. The two churches are aligned in a row east – west and are linked by later walling, giving the impression of a single very long building. The W church is the older. Its W wall with the massive lintelled door may date from the 10th or 11th century and the rest of the church from the 12th. The E church is medieval with a decorated 15th-century E window. A stone with two carved crosses leaning against the W church's E wall (exterior) is an early grave-marker. To the SW, higher up the mountain, is St Bline's holy well.

O Davies in *Co Louth Archaeol J* 9 no 2 (1938), 77-86; Gwynn and Hadcock 1970, 321.

32 Kilnasaggart Pillar Stone (J063150)

1¼ miles (2 km) S of Jonesborough, close to the Louth border in Edenappa

82, 83 Kilnasaggart Pillar Stone.

townland. Park at the road and approach through fields. A tall granite pillar marks the site of an early cemetery on one of Early Christian Ireland's great 'main roads', the *Slighe Miodhluachra*, running from Drogheda N through the Moyry Pass to Dunseverick in N Antrim. The long Irish inscription on the pillar's SE face records the dedication of the place by Ternohc son of Ceran Bic under the patronage of Peter the Apostle. Ternohc's death is recorded in the annals at 714 or 716 and the pillar can be reasonably dated to about 700. There are also three crosses on the SE face and ten on the NW. Excavation in 1966 and 1968 uncovered an Early Christian cemetery with both stone-built and dug graves, orientated E-W, near the pillar. Several small cross-carved slabs at the site may have served as grave-markers. The site was unenclosed in the mid 19th century; the present enclosure dates from early in this century.

W Reeves in *Ulster J Archaeol* 1 (1853), 221-5; publication by A Hamlin in a future volume of *Ulster J Archaeol*.

33   Lisbanemore Cashel (J078201)
4 miles (6·4 km) S of Newry, close to (E of) the A1 road, in Killeen townland. A large cashel, diameter about 55 m, with ruined wall 3 to 4·5 m thick at its base, partly removed on S side. This was a farmstead enclosure of the Early Christian period though no structures survive in the interior above ground.

34   Lisdoo Cashel (J081210)
In Killeen townland, ⅝ mile (1 km) N of Lisbanemore. A similar but rather smaller enclosure. Oval cashel, about 34·5 by 39 m, with a well-preserved surrounding wall, partly rebuilt on its N side. A souterrain is reported in this cashel but is not visible.

35   Lisnamintry Rath (J046544)
2 miles (3·2 km) E of Portadown and 3 miles (4·8 km) SW of Lurgan, approached from the lane to NE by a path across three fields. This rath, originally probably of bivallate form, has a circular central area with a perimeter bank, surrounded by a wide ditch, with remains of an outer bank and ditch. A gap to N probably marks the entrance.

36   Tynan Village Cross (H765430)
At the road junction W of Tynan parish church. On or near the site of the hilltop parish church was an Early Christian monastery associated with St Vindic. Little is known of its early history but two stone crosses survive, the Village Cross and the Terrace Cross now at Tynan Abbey (not in State Care), as well as fragments built into the graveyard wall. The Village Cross

is not in its original position, having been moved at least twice. It is composite, made up of two different crosses, the base and lower shaft of one being matched with the upper shaft and head of another. The lower shaft on the E side has a rectangular panel with Adam and Eve and on the W side is another panel with a large figure and smaller figures behind. The head is mended and partly reconstructed, of open ringed form decorated with tall bosses. The shaft has panels of interlaced decoration. On the nearby graveyard gatepost is an unusual hollowed stone, a 17th-century sundial, of which another example can be seen in Monaghan town.

W Reeves in *J Roy Soc Antiq Ireland* 16 (1883-4), 412-30; H Roe in *Seanchas Ardmhacha* 1 no 2 (1955), 112-13.

MEDIEVAL MONUMENTS

37 Armagh Friary (H876447)

At the SE edge of Armagh, reached by the drive off the ring-road which leads to the District Council offices (former archbishop's palace). Remains of the Franciscan friary church, founded by Archbishop O'Scannail in 1263-4. It had prominent patrons and played an important part in the city's religious life until it was suppressed in 1542. Some religious life continued, but the buildings were involved in warfare later in the 16th century and were ruined by 1600. Since then they have been robbed for stone. The surviving remains are of the 13th-century church, 49·8 m long (the longest known friary church in Ireland). The W end survives to a good height with a W door, and two arches (one partly reconstructed) open S into a missing aisle. Further E the church is more ruined, perhaps as a result of the fall of the tower, added in the 15th century at the junction of nave and chancel. Two empty graves and two tomb recesses near the E end are reminders of the important patrons buried in the friary church, including Gormlaith O'Donnell, wife of Domhnall O'Neill, in 1353. The cloister N of the church has almost entirely disappeared but excavation in the 1960s showed traces of medieval occupation further N, near the ring-road.

Gwynn and Hadcock 1970, 242; C J Lynn in *Ulster J Archaeol* 38 (1975), 61-80; DOENI guide-card (1977).

85   Armagh Friary from the south-west.

38 Moyry Castle (J057146)

7½ miles (12 km) SSW of Newry, in Carrickbroad townland, close to no 32

86 *Moyry Castle.*

(Kilnasaggart), approached uphill under the railway bridge to w. The castle is set on a rocky height, overlooking the strategically important Moyry Pass (Gap of the North). The small tower, three storeys high, has rounded corners, gun-loops and a machicolation over the door. Fragmentary remains of the bawn wall survive. The castle was built in 1601 to secure the pass during Mountjoy's northern campaign.

PSAMNI (1940), 79; Hayes-McCoy 1964, 2.

LATER MONUMENT

39 Castledillon Obelisk (H909494)
On the summit of Cannon Hill, in Turcarra townland, reached by a minor road N off the A3, then an uphill walk. Castle Dillon, former home of the Molyneux family, is to the SE. Tall, tapering shaft, a prominent landmark, with an inscription recording its erection in 1782 by Sir Capel Molyneux 'to commemorate the glorious revolution, which took place in favour of the constitution of the Kingdom, under the auspices of the volunteers of Ireland'.

County Down

PREHISTORIC MONUMENTS

40   Annadorn Dolmen (J429459)

5½ miles (8·8 km) SE of Ballynahinch, on the NE shore of Loughinisland Lake, within sight of no 73, Loughinisland Churches. A slightly displaced capstone covers a rectangular chamber of which three side stones survive. An early account suggests that this was formerly set in a large circular cairn and approached by a lintelled passage, so it may be the remains of a passage grave.

ASCD (1966), 78.

87   Audleystown Cairn.

4

41 Audleystown Cairn (J562504)

87 Near the s shore of Strangford Lough, NW of Castleward, approached from a turning off the A25 and across fields. Dual court grave, discovered in 1946 and excavated in 1952. The trapezoidal long cairn, its sides revetted with dry-stone walling, has a shallow forecourt at each end opening into four-chambered galleries. Remains of 34 skeletons, partly burned, were found during excavation, as well as Neolithic pottery and flint implements.

A E P Collins in *Ulster J Archaeol* 17 (1954), 7-56 and 22 (1959), 21-25.

88 **42 Ballynoe Stone Circle** (J481404)

2½ miles (4 km) s of Downpatrick, reached by a long footpath w off the minor road s from Downpatrick to Rathmullan, near the disused railway station. This large, complex monument was partly excavated in 1937-8 but its development and date are still not entirely clear. The site appears now as a large circle of closely-spaced stones with some outliers, surrounding an oval mound. The E part of the mound has a stone kerb and there is an arc of stones beyond its w end. Excavation uncovered a rectangular stone cist at each end of the mound with cremated bones. The site as we see it is probably the result of a long development, and a late Neolithic to earlier Bronze Age date range is likely.

ASCD (1966), 87-89; W Groenman-van Waateringe and J J Butler in *Palaeohistoria* 18 (1976), 73-110.

88   Ballynoe Stone Circle.

43 Dunnaman Court Grave (J289151)

1⅛ miles (1·5 km) WNW of Kilkeel, approached on a footpath N from the A2 beside the parochial house at Massfort. The unusually long burial gallery is built of split granite and surviving jamb stones suggest there were originally four segments. No sign survives of court stones or a cairn.

ASCD (1966), 73-4.

44 The Giant's Ring (J327677)
¾ mile (1·2 km) s of Shaw's Bridge, off the Ballylesson road in Ballynahatty townland, close to an early crossing over the river Lagan. Large carpark at entrance. The circular enclosure is over 180 m in diameter, its bank 3·6 m high and 18·2 m wide, made of material dug from the interior. There are now five gaps in the bank. Just E of centre is a chambered grave of five uprights with a large capstone, possibly the remains of a passage grave. The date and function of the monument are both difficult to establish. It *may* be a late Neolithic ceremonial or assembly site.

A E P Collins in *Ulster J Archaeol* 20 (1957), 44-50; *ASCD* (1966), 89-91.

89   *The Giant's Ring, chambered grave with bank beyond.*

45 Goward Dolmen (J244310)
2⅓ miles (3·7 km) NE of Hilltown, ¼ mile (0·4 km) s of the B8 Castlewellan-Hilltown road. Portal dolmen, locally known as Cloughmore Cromlech or Pat Kearney's Big Stone. The huge granite capstone has slipped from its original position over a rectangular chamber. Stones at the E end suggest a curving façade, allied to the court grave tradition.

ASCD (1966), 79-80.

46 Kilfeaghan Dolmen (J232154)
3⅞ miles (6·2 km) ESE of Rostrevor, reached by a lane N off the A2 just W of the Causeway Water and a path across two fields. Portal grave at the N end of

90 *Goward Dolmen.*   91 *Kilfeaghan Dolmen.*

a long cairn, once much larger than is now visible, extending N as well as S of
the dolmen. The enormous granite capstone is estimated to weigh some 35
tons and may have been an erratic boulder already on the site, undermined
and propped up with portal and side stones to form this spectacular dolmen.
Excavation early in this century discovered bone and pottery.

A E P Collins in *Ulster J Archaeol* 22 (1959), 31-2; *ASCD* (1966), 80-81.

47 **Legananny Dolmen** (J288434)

4 miles (6·4 km) S of Dromara and 5 miles (8 km) NW of Castlewellan on the

92 *Legananny Dolmen.*

s side of Slieve Croob, with a magnificent view of the Mourne Mountains. This famous tripod dolmen has a large flat capstone gracefully balanced on three unusually tall supporting stones. Slight traces remain of a cairn which must once have been far more extensive. There is an early record of urns found in the dolmen.

ASCD (1960), 81.

48   Millin Bay Cairn (J629495)

2¼ miles (3·6 km) SE of Portaferry in Keentagh townland, close to the E coast of the Ards peninsula overlooking Millin Bay, approached along a fenced path from the coast road. This complex late Neolithic burial monument appears now as an oval mound of sand, grass-grown, with a surrounding oval stone setting. Excavation in 1953 revealed a complicated sequence   9 of structures under the mound. Earliest was a N-S stone wall, followed by a long stone cist with the bones of at least 15 individuals, neatly sorted and stacked. Around this and another cist an oval of stone slabs was set, externally supported by a bank, and the oval area was infilled with shingle and slabs. Between the bank and the outer oval of stones seven more cists were inserted, some with cremated bone, and the whole area was finally covered with the long mound of sand we see today. Many of the stones were decorated with pecked curvilinear and rectilinear motifs. Finds were sparse but a late Neolithic date seems likely.

A E P Collins, D M Waterman and others, *Millin Bay, a late Neolithic cairn in county Down* (HMSO, 1955); *ASCD* (1966), 86-87.

EARLY CHRISTIAN PERIOD MONUMENTS

49   Derry Churches (J613524)

1½ miles (2·4 km) NE of Portaferry, E of the A2 to Cloghy, approached by a fenced path. Two small ruined churches stand on a rise in damp surroundings. There is written evidence of pre-Norman ecclesiastical activity on the site, associated with St Cummain, and there was a chapel here in 1306. The s church is smaller and earlier with *antae* to E and W, a W door and E and s   93 windows. The stone was originally bound with clay, not mortar, and there are cavities for scaffolding poles and horizontal intra-mural timbers in the walls. Some medieval alterations to the door and E window are marked by contrasting mortar. A 10th- or 11th-century date is possible, though a 12th-century one has also been suggested. The N church is larger, originally also built with clay, not mortar. It had a s door, an E window and perhaps a tower at the W end. A small early cross-carved stone is set in the N church.

93 Derry Churches, south church from the north-east.

Excavation in 1962 showed Early Christian occupation and a cemetery of stone-built graves under the churches, with an earlier building of stone and timber, perhaps a church, under the s church. Conservation following excavation included the straightening of the dangerously southward-leaning N wall of the smaller church and the replacing of the original clay bonding material with similarly coloured mortar.

ASCD (1966), 290-91; D M Waterman in *Ulster J Archaeol* 30 (1967), 53-75.

50   Dromore Cross (J200533)

At the approach to the bridge over the river Lagan, at the edge of the cathedral graveyard. The present cathedral must stand on or near the pre-Norman monastic site, associated with St Colman, and the cross survives from the early monastery. An inscription on the shaft records how it was re-erected in 1887, with much of the shaft and part of the head restored, after use elsewhere in the town as market cross and the base of the town stocks. Even in its fragmentary and weathered condition it is possible to appreciate the impressive scale of the granite cross and the delicacy of the decorated panels on its shaft. A cross-carved boulder, known as St Colman's Pillow, also probably from the early monastery, is now kept in the cathedral chancel.

E D Atkinson, *Dromore: an Ulster diocese* (Dundalk, 1925), 87-89; *ASCD* (1966), 274-5.

51 Drumadonnell Cross

Formerly built into the N gable of the school in Drumadonnell townland at J244393, but removed for safety when the school became derelict in the 1970s and re-erected freestanding and under cover in Historic Monuments and Buildings Branch stone store in Castlewellan Forest Park (J335365). Not ordinarily accessible to visitors except by arrangement with the Branch. Granite cross on tall, cubical base. The head is ringed but unpierced with a circular motif at the crossing on each face. Within the wide edge mouldings are panels of mainly interlaced decoration, partly badly weathered but partly still clear.

ASCD (1966), 301.

52 Drumena Cashel and Souterrain (J312340) 24, 25

2¼ miles (3·6 km) SW of Castlewellan, close to a minor road ESE off the A25 to Rathfriland, E of Lough Island Reavy. Oval cashel, the wall 2·7 to 3·6 m thick, partly rebuilt after excavation in 1925-6. The gap to the E may be the original entrance rather than the narrow modern approach gap. Confused stones in the S part of the enclosure seem to be remains of house foundations. In the SW area is a T-shaped souterrain (accessible), its walls of dry-stone construction and its roof lintelled (some lintels replaced in concrete). The original entrance to the souterrain was by its SE arm. Though not closely datable from excavated finds, this is clearly a farmstead enclosure of the Early Christian period. There are other cashels in this rocky upland area.

ASCD (1966), 176-7.

53 Lisnagade Fort (J086440) 22

3 miles (4·8 km) SW of Banbridge and 1¼ miles (2 km) ENE of Scarva. One of Northern Ireland's most impressive earthworks, a rath with three massive banks and ditches (trivallate). The original entrance to SE is marked by breaks in the banks and causeways over the ditches. To the N, linked by banks and ditches, is a small circular rath. Excavations in both enclosures in the early 1950s are not yet published. Part of the line of the Dane's Cast runs close by, S of the fort.

ASCD (1966), 149-50.

54 Lisnavaragh Fort (J081442)

⅜ mile (0·6 km) W of Lisnagade Fort, in Lisnagade townland, in the bend of a lane. Oval enclosure with three surrounding banks and two ditches (the outermost ditch is probably filled in). The original entrance through the substantial banks and ditches is from the E. The 1951 excavation is not yet published.

ASCD (1966), 150.

55   Maghera Church and Round Tower (J372342)

2 miles (3·2 km) NNW of Newcastle in Carnacavill townland, beside the Church of Ireland parish church. Gated drive from road leads to carpark at church. The ruined round tower marks the site of an early monastery founded by the 6th-century St Domongart (Donard), who gave his name to the highest peak in the Mourne Mountains. The tower stood to its full height until the early 18th century, when it fell in a great storm, and is now a stump 5·4 m high. It is built of local granite boulders and shale and has the usual raised doorway. Small-scale excavation in 1965 showed evidence of Early Christian occupation near the tower. In the oval graveyard E of the parish church (approached past the church) is the ruin of the medieval parish church, perhaps 13th century in date. It has a W door (unblocked during conservation work in the mid 1970s) and a small N window. A feature of the walls is voids left where horizontal intra-mural timbers have rotted away. At least two pre-Norman cross-carved stones survive in the graveyard.

ASCD (1966), 306-7; excavation report by A Hamlin in a future volume of *Ulster J Archaeol*.

94   Maghera Round Tower.

On Mahee Island, reached by twisting lanes and causeways off the A22 s of Comber. Small carpark at the site. The best example in Northern Ireland of a pre-Norman monastic enclosure with its buildings. Nendrum is associated with St Mochaoi who died at the end of the 5th century, but references to the monastery begin in the 7th and continue until a fire in 976, perhaps a Viking raid, when the abbot was burned in his house. In the late 12th century a small Benedictine monastic cell was founded on the site, but by 1306 the parish church was here, abandoned for Tullynakill on the mainland in the 15th century. The site was extensively excavated by H C Lawlor in 1922-4 when enclosure walls, church and round tower were restored. The glacial hill is crowned with three concentric walled enclosures, irregularly oval in plan. Little is known of the outer cashel, only partly in State Care. In the middle cashel on the sw side are circular hut foundations, which excavation suggested were craft workshops, and a rectangular building known as the 'schoolhouse', also a workshop. In the inner cashel were the most important buildings, including the church with its graveyard and the base of a round tower NW of the church. The W wall of the church was reconstructed in the 1920s, incorporating cross-carved stones for safety and a reconstructed

95   Nendrum Sundial.

95   sundial at the SW corner. Finds from the 1920s excavation are on show in the Ulster Museum.

H C Lawlor, *The monastery of St Mochaoi of Nendrum* (Belfast, 1925); *ASCD* (1966), 292-5; Gwynn and Hadcock 1970, 42, 107.

21   **57   Rough Fort** (J142604)
⅓ mile (0·5 km) W of Moira at the roadside in Risk townland. Well-preserved, unexcavated rath. The high central area is slightly dished, surrounded by a deep ditch, a bank and outer ditch, much silted up and partly occupied by the road. A causeway on the E side gives access to the central area.

40, 41   **58   St John's Point Church** (J527338)
1½ miles (2·4 km) SSW of Killough, near the SE tip of the Lecale peninsula on the road to St John's Point lighthouse. This small church, probably of the 10th or 11th century, may mark the site of an early monastery associated with Eoan (John) son of Cairland, but in medieval times it was a chapel. It is an excellent example of a small, pre-Romanesque church with lintelled W door with sloping jambs, *antae* to E and W and a S window. This stone church was almost certainly preceded by a wooden church. Small-scale excavation in 1978 discovered burials under the N wall but no sign of the claimed radial arrangement of graves around the church.

ASCD (1966), 295; N F Brannon in *Ulster J Archaeol* 43 (1980), 59-64.

59   Woodgrange Rath and Tower-House (J444466)
3½ miles (5·6 km) S of Crossgar, 1 mile (1·6 km) NE of Annadorn Dolmen (no 40). Platform rath on hilltop with the remains of a tower-house on its NW side. This is a stretch of wall 3·6 m long with one splayed loop. Another rath with an added tower-house can be seen (not in State Care) at Castle-skreen (J466400) in the Lecale peninsula.

ASCD (1966), 255.

MEDIEVAL MONUMENTS

96   **60   Ardtole Church** (J564382)
¾ mile (1·2 km) NE of Ardglass, E of the A2, on a hilltop overlooking the sea and the Isle of Man. An early cross slab from this site, now built into the church at Chapeltown, and a souterrain recorded S of the church suggest Early Christian activity on the hilltop. The ruin is of the medieval parish church, traditionally abandoned after a massacre. The long narrow church seems largely of 15th-century date, with a huge E window and opposed N

96   Ardtole Church looking east.

and s doors, one with a draw-bar hole.

F J Bigger in *J Roy Soc Antiq Ireland* 46 (1916), 130-135; *ASCD* (1966), 298.

61   Audley's Castle (J578506)

97

1 mile (1·6 km) NW of Strangford in Castleward townland, on a rocky height overlooking Strangford Lough, signposted from the Downpatrick to Strangford (A25) road. 15th-century tower-house built by the Audley family but passing to the Wards in 1646 and used in 1738 as an eye-catching

97   Audley's Castle.

focus of the long vista along Castle Ward's Temple Water. Though the bawn is ruined low its full circuit can be traced, running s to the cliff edge. The tower-house, like Kilclief, is of 'gatehouse' type with two projecting towers linked by a high arch (machicolation) to defend the entrance. In one tower were latrines and in the other a spiral stair leads to first and second floor rooms and the roof. The first floor room has a reconstructed wooden floor and semicircular stone barrel vault. The tower is well-provided with cupboards, window-seats, latrines and drain holes for slops.

48, 49

ASCD (1966), 225-227; DOENI guide-card (with Strangford and Portaferry) (1980).

62 Clough Castle (J409403)

44,45

At the junction of the A25 and A24 in Clough village, in a strategically important site with commanding views. Excellent example of an Anglo-Norman earthwork castle with added stone tower. A small kidney-shaped bailey lies s of a large mound, originally separated from it by a 2·1 m deep ditch. Excavation on the mound's summit in 1950 showed that originally (late 12th or very early 13th century) there was a timber palisade round the summit with pits for archers within. The foundation of a long rectangular hall was found in the NE half of the area, probably built in the mid 13th century, and later in the century a small rectangular stone keep was built to the sw. This survives, two storeys high, and was conserved in 1981-2. In the late Middle Ages, apparently after a period of disuse, it was restored and added to, resulting in an L-shaped tower-house.

D M Waterman in *Ulster J Archaeol* 17 (1954), 103-163; *ASCD* (1966), 200-203.

63 Downpatrick Mound (J483450)

98

On the NW outskirts of Downpatrick, on the edge of the Quoile marshes, approached by a path leading N from Mount Crescent. Known as the Mound of Down, English Mount and Rathkeltair, this is one of the major earthworks of Northern Ireland, consisting of an egg-shaped enclosure, defined by a steep bank and wide outer ditch. In the SE part of the interior is a tall, U-shaped mound with its own surrounding ditch. The large earthwork may be a pre-Norman enclosure, reused as the site of an Anglo-Norman castle mound of the invasion period, but the monument remains somewhat enigmatic. Work on clearance and presentation is under way in 1982.

Irish Naturalists Journal 6 (1936-7), 118; *ASCD* (1966), 202-3.

64 Dromore Mound (J206531)

43

In Ballyvicknacally townland on the E outskirts of Dromore, on the s side of

98

Mount Street. The mound lies in a bend of the river Lagan with extensive views along the valley. The best-preserved and most impressive example in Ulster of an Anglo-Norman motte and bailey castle. The mound rises 12·2 m high above its encircling ditch, blocking the landward approach from the N. To the S is the small, squarish bailey above the river. An outer bank and ditch provide further protection to E, N and NW. Excavation on the motte in 1951 showed that the first summit defence was a timber palisade, followed by the low bank which is still visible.

D M Waterman in *Ulster J Archaeol* 17 (1954), 164-8; *ASCD* (1966), 203-4.

98 *Downpatrick Mound, air view.*

65 **Dundrum Castle** (J404369)

VIII
99

On a wooded hill NW of Dundrum village with fine views over sea, mountains and inland. Large carpark below the castle. Probably fortified in pre-Norman times, this hilltop was chosen by John de Courcy in or soon after 1177 for one of his coastal castles, dominating Dundrum Bay. Captured by King John in 1210, the castle passed to the Earls of Ulster in 1227 but in the later Middle Ages was in Irish hands (the Magennises). The earliest stone castle was the polygonal upper ward on the highest part of the hill with surrounding rock-cut ditches. The circular keep was soon added (its upper parts rebuilt in the 15th century) and the twin-towered gatehouse later in the 13th century. The date of the added polygonal lower ward is uncertain: suggestions range from the 13th to the 15th century. Latest is the

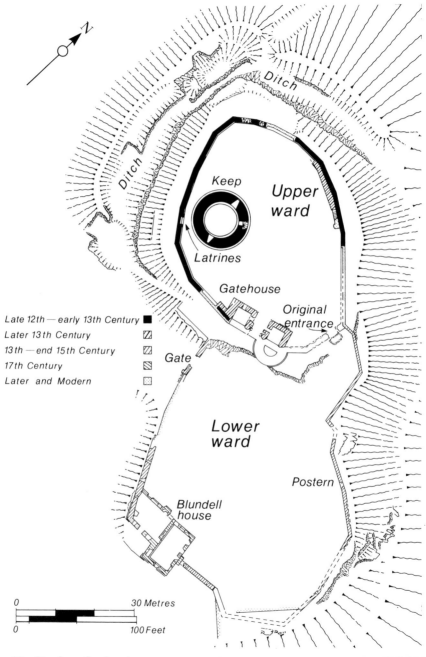

Late 12th — early 13th Century ■
Later 13th Century ▨
13th — end 15th Century ▨
17th Century ▨
Later and Modern ▦

N

Ditch

Ditch

Keep

Upper ward

Latrines

Gatehouse

Original entrance

Gate

Lower ward

Postern

Blundell house

0   30 Metres
0   100 Feet

99   *Dundrum Castle, plan.*

VIII *Dundrum Castle (Down).*

IX Inch Abbey (Down).

...encastle with rock-cut ditch in foreground (Down).

XI *Hillsborough Fort Gatehouse (Down)*.

house in the sw corner, built by the Blundell family in the 17th century, now a tall, gaunt ruin but once a grand dwelling.

D M Waterman in *Ulster J Archaeol* 14 (1951), 15-29 and 27 (1964), 136-9; *ASCD* (1966), 207-211; DOENI guide-card (1977).

66 Duneight Motte and Bailey (J278608)

2⅓ miles (3·8 km) s of Lisburn and ⅝ mile (1 km) E of Ravernet. Anglo-Norman motte and bailey strategically sited on the N bank of the Ravernet river to command the valley route. The motte is triangular, separated from the bailey by a ditch. The bailey is a truncated oval in plan, protected by a ditch and bank and an extra ditch to the E , but on the river side (s) the defences are less formidable. Excavation in 1961 showed that the bailey was a remodelled pre-Norman enclosure. Parts of wooden and stone buildings were found in this enclosure and slighter structures outside to the E. It can probably be identified with *Dún Echdach*, mentioned in the annals in 1003 and in 1010, when a distinction was made between the *dún* (fort) and *baile* (perhaps the settlement outside). Excavation also uncovered a collared urn with a cremation burial, evidence of Bronze Age activity beside the river.

D M Waterman in *Ulster J Archaeol* 26 (1963), 55-78; *ASCD* (1966), 205-6.

67 Greencastle (J247119)   X

4 miles (6·4 km) sw of Kilkeel, reached by minor roads off the A2 from Kilkeel or Lisnacree and down a drive to carpark at the castle. Prominently sited on a rocky outcrop close to Greencastle Point, the castle commands the narrow entry to Carlingford Lough and is within sight of Carlingford Castle. A royal castle, built in the 13th century, it had an eventful military history. Besieged and taken by Edward Bruce in 1316, attacked and spoiled by the Irish at least twice in the later 14th century, it was still maintained as a garrison for Elizabeth in the 1590s. Part of the area is now occupied by a working farm. The castle is approached across an impressive rock-cut ditch, partly excavated and left open. The curtain wall with four corner towers enclosed a trapezoidal area but is badly ruined. Part of the E curtain, found collapsed intact into the ditch, is reconstructed near the carpark. The large rectangular keep is of the 13th century but with substantial 15th- and 16th-century alterations. It was originally entered by a first floor door on the s, protected by a forebuilding (excavated foundations visible). A ground floor door in the w wall is a 15th-century alteration and the rough gap near the SE angle is a late forced entry. The cross walls dividing the ground floor into three vaults are also 15th-century insertions. At first floor level was the great hall (late medieval windows and fireplace) with a latrine in the NE corner. The upper parts of the keep, with mural passages, wall-walks and angle turrets, are a 15th-century remodelling. Fragments of other buildings in the ward include part of a long rectangular structure sw of the keep. A

long series of excavations has been done in connection with a substantial conservation programme.

D M Waterman in *Ulster J Archaeol* 15 (1952), 87-102; *ASCD* (1966), 211-219; C Gaskell-Brown in *Ulster J Archaeol* 42 (1979), 51-65; C J Lynn, forthcoming.

53 68 Grey Abbey (J583682)

On the E edge of Greyabbey village, beside the Rosemount estate, with a carpark at the entrance. With Inch Abbey the best example of Anglo-Norman Cistercian architecture in Ulster, daughter-house of Holm Cultram (Cumbria), founded in 1193 by John de Courcy's wife, Affreca. Poor and decayed in the late Middle Ages, the abbey was dissolved in 1541, but in the early 17th century was granted to Sir Hugh Montgomery and the nave was refurbished for parish worship until the late 18th century. The remains, in their beautiful parkland setting, consist of the church with cloister and surrounding buildings to the S. The church, entered through an elaborate W
100 door, has an aisleless nave, transepts with two chapels in each and a short chancel lit by tall lancet windows. The buildings round the cloister include a once fine aisled chapter house and a still impressive refectory with reader's pulpit, but the W range and cloister walks have disappeared. The three buttresses propping the S wall of the nave are part of a major conservation programme done early in this century.

ASCD (1966), 275-9; DOENI guide-card (1979).

Grey Abbey, west door of church.

Holywood Motte (J401795)
On the N side of Brook Street, in Ballykeel townland, originally overlooking Belfast Lough. Anglo-Norman castle mound, formerly probably with a ditch round its base and a timber palisade round the summit, but now with a spiral path and tree-planted, the result of 19th-century landscaping. King John stayed at Holywood in 1210 and a castle here is mentioned in 1234.

ASCD (1966), 194.

70 Inch Abbey (J477455)
¾ mile (1·2 km) NW of Downpatrick, reached by a turning off the A7 and lane to a carpark at the entrance. This beautiful site, on the N bank of the Quoile, was originally an island in the Quoile Marshes. A pre-Norman monastery here, called *Inis Cumhscraigh*, was plundered by Vikings in 1002. Its large earthwork enclosure has been traced from air photos. The visible remains are of the Cistercian abbey, daughter-house of Furness (Lancs), founded in the 1180s by John de Courcy in atonement for his destruction of Erenagh, 3 miles (4·8 km) to the S. The Cistercian precinct was enclosed by a bank and ditch and is mostly in State Care, extending N to S from the parish graveyard to the river and E to W up the valley sides. The buildings are mainly of the late 12th and 13th centuries. The church had an aisled nave,   IX
transepts with pairs of chapels, and a chancel lighted, like Grey Abbey, by graceful grouped lancet windows. In the 15th century, when the monastic community was smaller, the church was altered: by walling in the chancel and first bay of the nave and blocking off the transepts, a much smaller church was created and the rest was abandoned. The cloister walks to the S have disappeared but foundations of the E and S ranges remain, as well as outlying buildings towards the river. These include an infirmary and a bakehouse with a well nearby.

ASCD (1966), 279-81; A Hamlin in *Ulster J Archaeol* 40 (1977), 85-88; DOENI guide-card (1983).

71 Jordan's Castle, Ardglass (J559372)   101
In Ardglass, between Kildare Street and Quay Street, commanding the harbour. 15th-century tower-house, largest of the impressive group which testifies to the importance of Ardglass as a town and port in the Middle Ages. The characteristic projecting towers with a high machicolation arch face N. The entrance is protected by a smaller machicolation at right angles to the main arch. The W tower contains a spiral stair and the E tower latrines at two levels. The ground floor chamber has a semicircular barrel vault with impressions of wicker centering. There are three chambers above, all with modern wooden ceilings. The antiquarian Francis Joseph Bigger bought the castle in 1911 and restored it, fitting it out with furniture and bequeathing it to the State in 1926. The figure corbels on the third floor are

101 Jordan's Castle, Ardglass, in about 1900.

modern copies of 14th-century figures in St Francis's Priory, Kilkenny.
The present flat roof is also modern: originally the roof was gabled.

ASCD (1966), 223-5; guide book (HMSO, 1963); DOENI guide-card (1977).

V **72 Kilclief Castle** (J597457)
2½ miles (4 km) s of Strangford on the A2, facing the sea. Carpark opposite.
Tower-house reputedly built by John Sely, bishop of Down, between 1413
and 1441. If this attribution is correct, this is the earliest datable tower-
house in county Down. Its features include the high machicolation arch
between projecting towers and stepped battlements. The machicolation
protects the entrance leading to a spiral stair in the SE tower. In the NE
tower is a latrine shaft with access from three of the four floors. As at
Jordan's Castle, the ground floor chamber has a semicircular barrel vault
built on wicker centering. On the second floor a 13th-century coffin-lid
from a nearby church was reused as a lintel for the fireplace. The two-light
window in the E wall is a modern reconstruction based on a surviving
fragment.

ASCD (1966), 233-5.

73 Loughinisland Churches (J424454)
In Tieveňadarragh townland, 4 miles (6·4 km) W of Downpatrick and 1
mile (1·6 km) E of the A24 Belfast to Newcastle road. Now reached by a
causeway, this was originally an island in the lake. A remarkable group of
three ruined churches stands in a large graveyard overlooking the lake. The
ᵣliest recorded reference is to a parish church here in 1306. The Middle

102　Loughinisland Churches, north church.

Church is the oldest, probably of the 13th century, with a draw-bar hole to secure the door. The large North Church was built in the 15th century, 102 probably to replace the Middle Church, and continued in use until 1720. Smallest and latest is the South (MacCartan's) Church. Its elaborately carved W door has the date 1636 and initials PMC for Phelim MacCartan. The MacCartans had one of their chief seats near the lake and this was probably their principal burial ground.

ASCD (1966), 305-6.

74　Mahee Castle (J524639)

Commanding the N end of Mahee Island in Strangford Lough, now reached by causeway. Visitors should park at Nendrum (no 56) and walk back to the castle. This tower-house, built in 1570 by an English soldier, Captain Browne, is badly ruined but still of considerable interest. Rectangular and fairly small in ground plan, it has two ground floor rooms, the larger with a semicircular vault built on plank centering and the smaller with a pointed vault probably built on paired wicker mats. The smaller room may have been a secure boat bay, important on an island site (compare nearby Sketrick, no 81). There were two storeys above, but the upper parts are ruined. Part of the bawn wall survives to the SW.

ASCD (1966), 244-5.

75 Movilla Abbey (J504744)

1 mile (1·6 km) E of Newtownards, on the S side of the B172 to Millisle, approached from the S through the large graveyard. This hilltop was occupied by one of Ulster's most important monasteries and scholarly centres, associated with the 6th-century St Finnian. Plundered by Vikings in 824, it was refounded in the 12th century as an abbey of Augustinian Canons, and survived until the suppression of religious houses in the 1540s. One stone only survives from the pre-Norman monastery: a slab with a sharply-cut ringed cross and an inscription asking for a prayer for Dertrend, *or do Dertrend*. The ruined church is long and narrow, its S wall largely lacking and N wall much rebuilt. It is partly 13th and partly 15th century in date. The altered E window has plain intersecting tracery, later blocked, incorporating an earlier, small, semicircular-headed window. In the W gable is a two-light transomed 15th-century window with carved decoration. Built into the inside of the N wall is the best collection in the north of 13th-century coffin-lids with foliate crosses. Shears indicate a woman's burial and a sword a man's. The pre-Norman slab is at the W end of the row.

54

ASCD (1966), 283-4; Gwynn and Hadcock 1970, 188.

VI 76 Narrow Water Castle (J127193)

5 miles (8 km) SE of Newry beside the A2 to Warrenpoint, picturesquely and strategically sited on a promontory in the Newry River. Tower-house and bawn, built in the 1560s at a cost of £361 4s 2d for an English garrison but later in Magennis hands. The tower entrance in the W wall was protected by a forebuilding and a corbelled machicolation above, with a murder-hole immediately inside. There are chambers at three levels with an attic, and straight stairs, latrine and other small chambers in the wall thickness. The first floor room has a semicircular barrel vault built on wicker centering. The present roof and some windows are restorations of the 1960s, and wicker centering from that restoration has been left in position in two windows to demonstrate this characteristically Irish method of construction. The bawn wall has been modified by later use but must represent the extent of the original enclosure, with part of the promontory to the W left for a small boat quay.

Guide book (HMSO, 1962); *ASCD* (1966), 241-3.

77 Newtownards Priory (J493738)

At the SE edge of the town, its tower a familiar landmark. These are the only substantial remains in Northern Ireland of a Dominican (Black) Friary, founded in the mid 13th century. The lower parts of the nave are of the 13th century, with two blocked doors in the S wall leading to the now-vanished cloister. Extensive 14th-century remodelling involved rebuilding ,ie upper parts of the nave, extending it westwards and adding a N aisle

106

reached through the surviving arcade. The friary was suppressed in 1541 and burned in 1572, but after the Plantation it was granted to Hugh, first Viscount Montgomery, who refurbished the church, rebuilding the N aisle and adding the tower. The elaborately decorated porch bears his initials HLM, but the soft Scrabo sandstone has weathered badly and much of the detail is unclear.

ASCD (1966), 284-7; Gwynn and Hadcock 1970, 228.

78   Portaferry Castle (J593509)

On the slope overlooking Portaferry harbour, within sight of Strangford and Audley's Castles across the lough. 16th-century tower-house, built by the Savage family. Simpler than the earlier 'gatehouse' type, it is square in plan with one projecting tower to the S. Here the entrance is defended by a small machicolation arch. Like early towers it has spiral stairs, but like some later ones lacks a stone vault, all the floors being originally of wood. The E angle is ruined and the castle is a shell.

ASCD (1966), 245-6; DOENI guide-card (with Audley's and Strangford Castles) (1980).

79   Quoile Castle (J497470)

1½ miles (2·4 km) NNE of Downpatrick, N of the A25, near the E bank of the Quoile river. Ruins of a late 16th-century tower-house, inhabited into the 18th century. The S angle has fallen, revealing an interesting cross-section through vaults and floors. On the ground floor were two chambers, each stone-vaulted, with many small gun-loops. A straight stair in the wall thickness led from the door to first floor level, and another to the second floor, both with fireplaces.

PLEASE NOTE: the castle is dangerous and should be viewed only from a distance until repaired.

ASCD (1966), 247-8.

80   Shandon Park Mound (J385728)

One of Belfast's few surviving medieval earthworks, reached by a path between numbers 45 and 47 Shandon Park in Knock. The mound, strategically sited on high ground with extensive views, is now conspicuous because planted with conifers. It is probably a motte, an Anglo-Norman castle mound, but the name *sean dún* (old fort) leaves open the possibility that this motte, like some others, was built on a pre-Norman fort site.

ASCD (1966), 194.

103 Sketrick Castle.

81 Sketrick Castle (J525625)

Island site off the w coast of Strangford Lough, now reached by a causeway, 5¾ miles (9·2 km) SE of Comber. Large tower-house, mentioned in written sources as involved in warfare in 1470, so perhaps built in the mid 15th century, but possibly later. It was actively involved in 16th-century warfare but stood fairly complete until 1896, when about half collapsed in a storm. It was four storeys high. There were four chambers at ground floor level, the largest with a vault built on wicker centering and two brick-lined recesses, probably ovens. The central space may have been a boat bay, and the small unlighted room could have been a lock-up or a treasury. Part of the bawn wall survives to N and E and a subterranean passage, roofed with stone lintels, provided a secure route out under the bawn wall to a freshwater spring, rising in a small chamber with a corbelled vault.

ASCD (1966), 250-52.

82 Strangford Castle (J589498)

On a height overlooking the harbour in Strangford town, across the strait from Portaferry Castle (no 78). Small tower-house, of the late 16th century in its present form, but a blocked door of 15th-century type at first floor level suggests remodelling of an earlier tower. The present entrance is a ~construction, positioned by the surviving corbelled machicolation above d a socket for a draw-bar to secure the original door. Of simple rectangu-

104   Strangford Castle.

lar plan, the castle has three floors with no stone vault and no sign of a stone stair. The first floor fireplace has an oven and dry 'keeping place'. There are pistol-loops at ground floor level and in the crenellations at roof level.

ASCD (1966), 252-3; D M Waterman in *Ulster J Archaeol* 30 (1967), 83-6; DOENI guide-card (with Audley's and Portaferry Castles) (1980).

PLANTATION PERIOD AND LATER MONUMENTS

83   Ballycopeland Windmill (J579761)

1 mile (1·6 km) W of Millisle on the B172. Carpark at the site. Windmills were once common in grain-growing E Down, but all except Ballycopeland are now ruined. Built probably in the 1780s, it was worked by the McGilton family until the 1914-18 war and from the 1950s to 1978 was restored to full working order. The mill is approached past the kiln house (which there are plans to restore). It is a tower mill, the cap with the sails moving on a 'dead curb' and kept into the eye of the wind by the fantail. The top floor has the hoppers into which the grain was emptied, falling to the stones floor below,

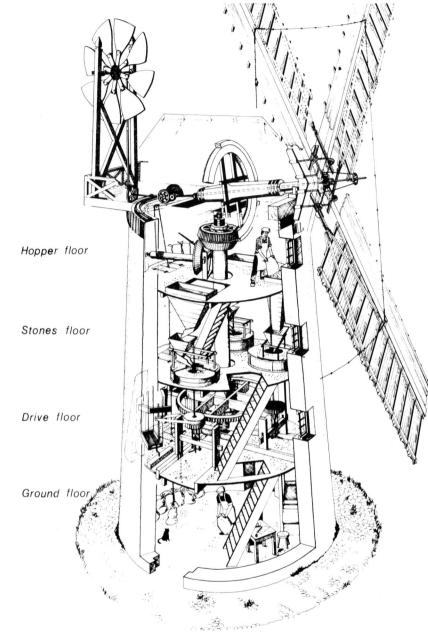

Hopper floor

Stones floor

Drive floor

Ground floor

105   *Ballycopeland Windmill, cutaway drawing.*

where there are three pairs of grind stones. Below again is the drive floor
where the drive from the central shaft is transferred to the stones, and finally
the ground floor where the grain began and ended its journey. Hulls were

110

collected in and cleared from the dust-house adjoining the mill.

PLEASE NOTE: the mill is not normally working for safety reasons. Special arrangements for its working have to be made with the Branch.

E R R Green, *The industrial archaeology of county Down* (1963), 53, fig 3; guide book (HMSO, 1962); DOENI guide-card (1979).

84 Hillsborough Fort (J245586)

106

Approached down a tree-lined avenue from the Square or from the Forest Park into the lake field SW of the fort. Artillery fort, built by Colonel Arthur Hill in the 1650s on the site of an Early Christian rath (excavated ditch 66 visible) to command important routes. Later in the century it held a royal garrison, but in the 18th and 19th centuries served a more peaceful purpose as a pleasure ground for the Hill family. The fort is square with spear-shaped angle bastions, the earth bank having its outer face revetted in stone. A rectangular gatehouse in the centre of the N side was remodelled in 1758 in XI a gothick style, with four corner towers and a battlemented parapet, and a new entrance in the NE side was given a gothick gazebo above. Extensive paths link the fort with the parish church (1760-74), the lake field and Hillsborough Forest Park.

ASCD (1966), 409-11; DOENI guide-card to Hillsborough (1977); C Gaskell-Brown and N F Brannon in *Ulster J Archaeol* 41 (1978), 78-87.

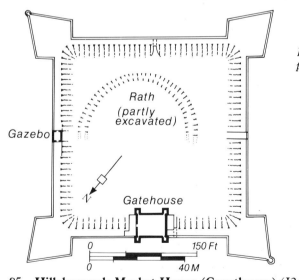

106   Hillsborough Fort, plan.

Rath (partly excavated)

Gazebo

Gatehouse

0   150 Ft

0   40 M

85 Hillsborough Market House (Courthouse) (J243586)

107

In the Square, built before 1765 as a market house, but now used as a courthouse. The first building had a two-storey square central block with single storey covered market arcades on each face. In about 1810 the N and S

107   Hillsborough Market House.

wings were added, together with the granite plinth, and sandstone details – cornices, urns and balls. A new clock and bell were installed in 1810.

ASCD (1966), 411-14; C E B Brett, *Mid Down* (Ulster Architectural Heritage Society, 1974), 14; DOENI guide-card to Hillsborough (1977).

111   **86   Hillsborough: Richhill Gates**
Facing the Market House at the entrance to Hillsborough Castle, moved here from Richhill House, county Armagh, in 1936. These fine wrought iron gates and screen were made probably by Cornish immigrants to Armagh, the Thornberry brothers of Falmouth, and were set up at Richhill in 1745. Areas of plain railings are contrasted with exuberantly decorated panels, with an 'overthrow' bearing a coat of arms. Repaired in 1936, a further major renovation was completed in 1976.

DOENI guide-card to Hillsborough (1977).

108   **87   Kirkistown Castle** (J646580)
1¼ miles (2 km) NNE of Cloghy, NW of the A2 coast road near Ringboy. Though its surroundings are badly scarred by quarrying, this remains a particularly fine example of a tower-house in its bawn. Traditionally built for Roland Savage in 1622, it post-dates the Plantation but is fully in the late medieval tower-house tradition. The entrance to the tower on its SE side is protected by a corbelled machicolation at roof level. There are three floors, the first floor main chamber having a pointed stone vault. Quoins, door and window dressings are in fine hard limestone. In about 1800 the tower was much altered in Gothic Revival style, acquiring large pointed sash windows, plaster ceilings, gothick fireplaces and new woodwork. Massive buttresses

112

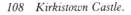

108 Kirkistown Castle.

were added to the SE face in the 19th century to counter some signs of instability. Parts of the bawn walls survive to NW and SE with three-quarter round flanker towers at the angles.

ASCD (1966), 238-41.

88 Struell Wells (J513442)

109

1½ miles (2·4 km) E of Downpatrick, signposted off the B1 (Ardglass) road and reached down a long, rough lane. The site is rich in traditions and strongly associated with St Patrick, but the earliest written reference is in 1306 and none of the surviving buildings is certainly earlier than about 1600. A fast-flowing stream runs, partly underground, through the secluded, rocky valley and along it are ranged five buildings. Furthest NW is the gaunt shell of a mid 18th-century church, apparently never finished. This must have replaced an earlier church: a chapel was listed here in the 1306 taxation roll. Nearby is the Drinking Well, circular with a domed vault built on wicker centering. The Eye Well is rectangular with a pyramidal corbelled roof. To the SE the stone-roofed Men's Bath-house has a dressing room with seats leading to the bath-room with its tank. A third room, also with seats, served as dressing room to the adjoining Women's Bath-house, now

113

109   Struell Wells: drinking well left, eye well and bath-houses beyond.

roofless. Pilgrimages to the site are well documented from the 16th to 19th centuries.

ASCD (1966), 310-11.

89   The White House, Ballyspurge (J643550)
¾ mile (1·2 km) SE of Cloghy, on a slope overlooking Slanes Bay, approached by a long lane through the caravan site to the S and on foot uphill from the end of the lane. Built probably in the 1640s by Patrick Savage, this

110   The White House, Ballyspurge.

gabled house combines defensive with more purely domestic features. Rectangular in plan and 1½ storeys high, it has thick walls with pistol-loops and stands within the remains of a bawn with a gatehouse, but the windows are large and the general appearance is domestic rather than defensive.

ASCD (1966), 256-9.

111   Richhill Gates (Arm) now at Hillsborough.

County Fermanagh

PREHISTORIC MONUMENT

112 **90 Drumskinny Stone Circle, Cairn and Alignment** (H201707)
4½ miles (7·2 km) N of Kesh, E of the minor road N to Castlederg. The site lies in upland bog and was drained after excavation in 1962. A circle 12·8 m in diameter is made up of 39 stones, and a small round cairn is associated with an alignment, 7·6 m long, of 24 stones. The stones are fairly small and some replaced after the excavation are clearly marked. Far smaller but of the same general type as Beaghmore circles (no 124), this site dates probably from the Bronze Age.

D M Waterman in *Ulster J Archaeol* 27 (1964), 23-30.

112   Drumskinny Stone Circle.

EARLY CHRISTIAN PERIOD AND MEDIEVAL MONUMENTS

91 Aghalurcher Church (H365314)
1½ miles (2·4 km) S of Lisnaskea. This is the site of an early monastery, founded probably in the 7th century by St Ronan, but the visible ruins are of the medieval parish church. This was substantial, as the foundations of the E end show, but it is badly ruined. The church was patronised by the Maguires, whose main burial place was here. There are many fine gravestones, some protected in the covered vault on the N side of the church.

G Dagg in *J Roy Soc Antiq Ireland* 24 (1894), 264-70; Hickey 1976, 62-66.

92 Devenish Monastic Site (H224469)

Island site at the S end of Lower Lough Erne, 1½ miles (2·4 km) down-stream from Enniskillen. A ferry runs from Trory Point, reached along the lane to the lough shore (carpark) from the junction of the B82 to Kesh with the A32 to Ballinamallard. Cruisers also run from Enniskillen and Castle Archdale. Most important of Lough Erne's many island monasteries, Devenish was founded in the 6th century by St Molaise. It was raided by Vikings in 837 and burned in 1157, but in the Middle Ages flourished as the site of the parish church and St Mary's Augustinian Priory. There are extensive low earthworks on the hillside, but the earliest buildings are St Molaise's House (a very small church) and the fine round tower close by, both with accomplished Romanesque decoration and of the 12th century. *Teampull Mór*, the lower church, is early 13th century with a beautifully-moulded S window. It was extended to the E in about 1300, and later 57 additions include a residential wing to the N and the Maguire Chapel to the S, with 17th-century heraldic slabs. St Mary's Augustinian Priory on the 113 hilltop is of the mid 15th and early 16th centuries, with church, tower and small N cloister. In its graveyard stands an unusual, intricately-carved high cross of the mid 15th century. In the thatched site museum (built 1976-8) some of the many loose stones are displayed and set in their historical context.

113 Devenish, St Mary's Priory from the west.

117

C A R Radford in *Ulster J Archaeol* 33 (1970), 55-62 (with further references); Hickey 1976, 71-77; D M Waterman in *Ulster J Archaeol* 42 (1979), 34-50; DOENI guide-card (1979).

93   Inishmacsaint (H165541)

Island near the W shore of Lower Lough Erne off Ross Point, 7½ miles (12 km) NW of Enniskillen off the A46. No ferry service but there is a jetty close to the site at the SE corner of the island. A monastery was founded here by St Ninnid in the 6th century, and the site was later used for the parish church and graveyard, being abandoned for the mainland only in the 18th century. The ruined church is of two main periods: the W end represents a small pre-Romanesque church of perhaps the 10th or 11th century, with a blocked W door, and the E end is an extension of about 1200, with a small S window altered in the 15th century. SW of the church is a tall unringed cross, the head separately worked and attached to the shaft by a mortice and tenon joint. The cross is plain except for slight traces of panels on the head and is difficult to date closely though it probably belongs to the early monastic (pre 12th-century) period.

114   Inishmacsaint Cross.

PSAMNI (1940), 153; Gwynn and Hadcock 1970, 38; DOENI guide-card (with White Island) (1983).

94   White Island Church and Figures (H175600)

In Castle Archdale Bay, near the E shore of Lower Lough Erne, reached from the B82. No regular ferry but a boat is sometimes available at the Marina in Castle Archdale Country Park. A small ruined church of about 1200 lies within the large earthwork enclosure of a pre-Norman monastery. Nothing is known of the early history of the monastery, but one early grave slab is exhibited at the site. The main feature of the church is its late Romanesque s door. The stone figures set up against the N wall pre-date the church, and may belong to an earlier church. Sinkings in the tops of the heads may have supported timbers. There has been much discussion of the symbolism of the figures. There is no doubt that they are Christian in significance, not pagan, and a 9th- or 10th-century date seems likely.

D Lowry-Corry, B C S Wilson and D M Waterman in *Ulster J Archaeol* 22 (1959), 59-66; Hickey 1976, 34-50; DOENI guide-card (with Inishmacsaint) (1983).

PLANTATION PERIOD MONUMENTS

95   Castle Balfour (H362337)

In Lisnaskea, at the edge of the parish graveyard W of the main street,

115   Castle Balfour from the graveyard.

approached through the graveyard. The castle was built from about 1618 onwards by the Scottish planter, Sir James Balfour, and shows clear Scottish influence in plan and details. It was altered in 1652 and damaged in 1689 but continued in occupation until the early 19th century. Major restoration was done in the 1960s. A wing formerly projecting E into the graveyard has disappeared. The surviving building is of T plan with the entrance through a dressed-stone projecting bay with gun-loops. On the ground floor are vaulted rooms and a kitchen with remains of a large fireplace and small oven. The main dwelling rooms were at first floor level and the stairs to rooms above are carried in a corbelled-out turret.

The Rt Hon the Earl of Erne in *Ulster J Archaeol* 2 (1896), 79-85; D M Waterman in *Ulster J Archaeol* 31 (1968), 71-76.

VII **96 Enniskillen Castle** (H231442)
On the SW corner of Enniskillen island, approached from the main street by Castle Street or Wesley Street. The first castle was built to command the Erne by Hugh Maguire in the early 15th century. The lower parts of the keep may date from that period. A focus of Irish resistance to the English in the 16th century, it was much involved in warfare and fell after an eight day siege in 1594. In 1607 Captain William Cole was appointed constable and refurbished and remodelled the castle. The keep was repaired and the watergate added (not in fact a gate but a tower fronting the Erne). In the late 18th century the complex was remodelled as the Castle Barracks. The keep houses the Fermanagh County Museum and the Regimental Museum of the Royal Inniskilling Fusiliers.

E M Jope in *Ulster J Archaeol* 14 (1951), 32-47; H Dixon, *Enniskillen* (Ulster Architectural Heritage Society, 1973); DOENI guide-card (1980).

116 Monea Castle.

120

97 Monea Castle (H164493)

3 miles (4·8 km) SE of Derrygonnelly, ½ mile (0·8 km) E of Monea Church of Ireland church, approached along a wooded drive through Castletown demesne. The finest of Fermanagh's Plantation castles, built from 1618-19 for Malcolm Hamilton. Captured in the 1641 rising, it was refurbished and used until gutted by fire in the mid 18th century. The walled bawn is much ruined. It has two flanker towers, the one beside the entrance once used for housing pigeons. The castle at the SE corner of the bawn survives almost to full height though lacking its roofs. The entrance front (W) has two circular towers capped with square chambers with crow-stepped gables, closely paralleled at Claypotts near Dundee. On the ground floor were vaulted rooms and a kitchen, with hall and chambers above. The castle is well provided with gun-loops. A clump of trees in the partly-drained lake to the S marks a crannog.

E M Jope in *Ulster J Archaeol* 14 (1951), 32-47; DOENI guide-card (1977).

98 Old Castle Archdale (H186599)

In Castle Archdale Forest Park, close to the junction of the B72 and B82 roads, near the E shore of Lower Lough Erne. Carpark nearby. The much ruined remains of a T-shaped house and bawn built for the English planter, John Archdale, on land granted in 1612. Captured in 1641, the castle was repaired but finally burned and abandoned in 1689. Little survives of the bawn except part of the S wall with its wall-walk and a semicircular-headed gate. Above this on the outside is a Latin inscription recording the construc- tion by John Archdale in 1615. The house is at the N end of the bawn, very fragmentary and heavily restored. Parts of the E gable and S wall survive, but the main fragment is the projecting N tower, three storeys high, which held a wooden stair, lit by narrow windows and defended through gun-loops. Generally English in design, there are signs of Scottish influence in the details of the bawn gateway.

D M Waterman in *Ulster J Archaeol* 22 (1959), 119-123.

99 Tully Castle (H126566)

On the W shore of Lower Lough Erne, 3 miles (4·8 km) N of Derrygonnelly, approached by a lane off the A46 lough shore road between Enniskillen and Belleek. Carpark at approach path. Beautifully sited on a hill overlooking the lough, the fortified house and bawn were built for the Scottish planter, Sir John Hume, following his land grant in 1610, but were captured, burned and abandoned in 1641. The rectangular bawn with four rectangular angle towers is ruined low to the W but survives to some height to the E. An interesting feature of the bawn is extensive original paving. The house survives to almost full height of two storeys with attics. The ground floor room is vaulted with a large fireplace. The main accommodation above was reached by a wooden stair against the E wall of the projecting entrance tower. The upper N angles are carried up as projecting circular towers, not built of cut stone, like Castle Balfour, but of rubble, originally plastered. The T-plan is Scottish in inspiration but the work was probably carried out by Irish masons. A major conservation programme is nearing completion in 1983.

69, 70

D M Waterman in *Ulster J Archaeol* 22 (1959), 123-126.

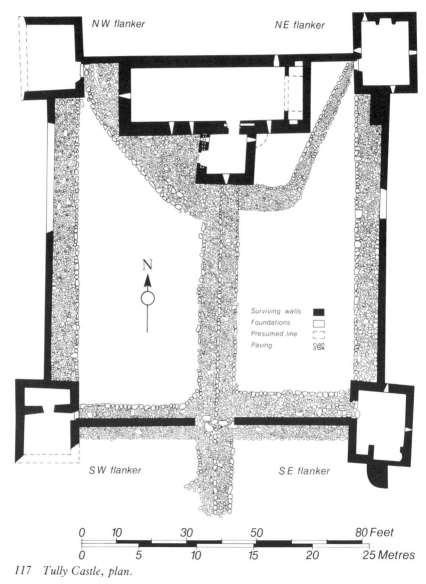

117   Tully Castle, plan.

County Londonderry

PREHISTORIC MONUMENTS

100   Ballybriest Dual Court Grave: Carnanbane (H762886) 118
On the lower W slopes of Slieve Gallion, overlooking Lough Fea, approached from the B41 SW from Draperstown or the B162 NW from Cookstown. Unfortunately damaged, cut almost in half down the long axis of the cairn. Originally at each end, E and W, a semicircular court led to a short, two-chambered burial gallery. Excavated in 1937, the site produced evidence for Neolithic activity, perhaps domestic occupation, under the cairn.

E E Evans in *Proc Roy Irish Acad* 45C (1939), 1-12.

118   Ballybriest Dual Court Grave from the west.

101   Ballybriest Wedge Grave (H762885)
Close to no 100, about 300 feet (91·5 m) to the S, downslope in bogland. Megalithic grave, only partly cut out of the peat, orientated to the SW, with two large capstones in place on side and end stones. It is difficult to be certain about its type, but a wedge grave seems likely.

PSAMNI (1940), 212.

119   Ballygroll: field wall and barrow during excavation.

102   Ballygroll Prehistoric Complex (C533137 and area)

6 miles (9·6 km) ESE of Londonderry, approached on the minor road N from Ervey crossroads to Highmoor and on foot up a long lane to the hilltop. A remarkable complex of prehistoric stone monuments survives, partly still covered by peat, on the summit of a sandy ridge. The features include at least the following: a court grave (furthest N) with a disturbed, cup-marked capstone, several wedge graves, two stone circles, a round cairn, a barrow, and many stretches of straight stone field walls. The date of the walls is uncertain but the megalithic monuments seem to extend from the Neolithic period into the Bronze Age. Excavation was done in 1978-9 on the barrow and a field wall in the context of land reclamation.

O Davies in *Ulster J Archaeol* 9 (1948), 48-53; B B Williams in *Ulster J Archaeol* 44-45 (1981-2), 29-46.

103   Ervey Court Grave (C517126)

3½ miles (5·6 km) NNW of Claudy and ⅓ mile (0·5 km) NNW of Ervey crossroads, E of a minor road. The remains of what was probably a court grave survive in a hollow at the SE corner of a field. There is one complete chamber to the W and part of a second to the E. The court would have opened to the E. Nos 102 and 106 are nearby.

PSAMNI (1940), 199.

104   Mobuy Standing Stone (H783859)

2 miles (3·2 km) SE of Ballybriest megaliths (nos 100 and 101), 1 mile (1·6 km) NNE of Lissan on the lower SW slopes of Slieve Gallion. A single stone stands on a level area on the hillside, according to memory the last of a

ring of eight or ten stones known as the Druids Circle.

105   Mount Sandel Mesolithic Site (C854307)

1¼ miles (2 km) SSE of Coleraine, close to the NE of the mound (no 115), between the woodland and 1970s housing. The area of the excavated Mesolithic occupation site is fenced and in 1982 awaits presentation work to remind visitors of the post-holes, pits and hearths of the 7th-millennium bc settlement.

P C Woodman in *Current Archaeology* 59 (1977), 372-376 and *Scientific American* 245 (1981), 120-132. Excavation report by P C Woodman forthcoming as HMSO monograph (1983).

106   Mullaboy Standing Stone (C516130)

⅓ mile (0·5 km) NNW of Ervey court grave (no 103) and 1¼ miles (2 km) ESE of Ballygroll (no 102), immediately W of a minor road. A tall *fallen* stone lies with its long axis N-S. Stones around it may be the remains of a cairn or result from field clearance, but without excavation it is impossible to be sure whether this was a solitary standing stone or part of a megalithic grave.

EARLY CHRISTIAN PERIOD AND MEDIEVAL MONUMENTS

107   Ballintemple Bullaun Stone (C810149)   39

2 miles (3·2 km) WSW of Garvagh on the B64 to Dungiven, beside the farmhouse immediately S of Errigal graveyard. This was the site of a pre-Norman church and the medieval parish church of Errigal. The bullaun stone must survive from the pre-Norman occupation: a large basalt boulder with a hollow, often water-filled and regarded as a font, but probably a mortar for grinding food and other materials. In the field N of the graveyard is a rock-cut souterrain (not in State Care), another sign of Early Christian activity in this area.

PSAMNI (1940), 197.

108   Banagher Church (C676066)

In Magheramore townland, 2 miles (3·2 km) SSW of Dungiven, approached from the B74 to Feeny or the minor road S from the centre of Dungiven through Turmeel. The church, on a prominent hill of sand and gravel, was traditionally founded by St Muiredach O'Heney who may have lived in the 11th or early 12th century. It is first mentioned in 1121. This was the medieval parish church, chosen by Archbishop Colton of Armagh as base for his visitation of Derry diocese in 1397, but abandoned in the 17th

120   Banagher Church: excavated east end showing altar and sacristy.

century. The nave must date from the early or mid 12th century (the date 474 on the W door was cut in the 1730s). There is a small semicircular-headed S window and a fine W door, archaic in general appearance, with a massive lintel and sloping jambs, but with a semicircular arch inside. The chancel was added in the early 13th century, with three windows, the S with elegant multiple roll mouldings, and a similarly moulded *sedile* (seat) in the S wall. This was blocked when the E end was remodelled in the 15th century to form a narrow sacristy behind the altar. Unfortunately after excavation the 15th-century features had to be covered again to prevent rapid weathering. The exterior E angles have attached shafts with decorated capitals, reset at a lower level than their original eaves height. SW of the chancel, in the same distinctive masonry, is the small church- or house-shaped mortuary house, traditionally St Muiredach's burial place. This is the source of the famous Banagher sand which can bring good fortune to members of the saint's family. E of the church is a simple stone cross and a bullaun stone (outside the graveyard wall), and a second cross stands across the road to the SW on the townland boundary. The foundation outside the graveyard gate is probably the remains of the medieval priest's strong-house or tower.

D M Waterman in *Ulster J Archaeol* 23 (1960), 82-88 and 39 (1976), 25-41; DOENI guide-card (with Bovevagh) (1983).

109   Bovevagh Church (C667141)
3 miles (4·8 km) NNW of Dungiven, reached by a turning W off the B192, on a hill above the Bovevagh river. This was the site of a pre-Norman church (a timber church – *dertech* – stood here in 1100) and of the medieval parish

51
58
120

121   Bovevagh Mortuary House.

church. The present church ruin is medieval with later alterations and was used until the 19th century. Near its SW corner is a small mortuary house or saint's grave, with a body-shaped cavity and hand-hole at the E end for access to the relics. Of rubble construction with a stone slab roof, it is simpler than the Banagher tomb but of the same general type. A third in the county can be seen at Tamlaghtard, E of Bellarena station (C677313), with a ruined medieval church and holy well nearby.

PSAMNI (1940), 200; D M Waterman in *Ulster J Archaeol* 23 (1960), 82-88; DOENI guide-card (with Banagher) (1983).

110   Drum Fort, also known as Larry's Fort (C654113)

2½ miles (4 km) NW of Dungiven, overlooking a tributary of the river Roe, approached on farm lanes. A large rath, perhaps originally bivallate, but now with a single bank to N, upslope, and a bank, ditch and outer bank to S, downslope. It is heavily overgrown and in 1982 awaits some clearance.

111   Dungiven Priory (C692083)

Reached on foot down a long lane SW from the A6 at the E approach to Dungiven. The graveyard and ruined church stand on a promontory high above the river Roe. A pre-Norman monastery associated with St Nechtan was succeeded in the 12th century by a priory of Augustinian Canons, closely associated with the O'Cahans who by the late Middle Ages had a castle on the site. After the suppression of the priory the buildings were remodelled in the early 17th century by Sir Edward Doddington to create a grand house and bawn, and the church was refurbished. The house had almost completely disappeared but was excavated in 1982. The church shows work of many periods. Earliest is the nave with its S window, contemporary with Banagher nave (early or mid 12th century). The fine chancel, originally stone-vaulted, was added in the 13th century and against its S wall is an ornate 15th-century tomb, traditionally of Cooey-na-Gall O'Cahan, who died in 1385. Though weathered and partly restored it is still impressive, by far the grandest tomb of its type in the north and probably by a western Scottish craftsman. There are traces of the early 17th-century refurbishing, especially in the chancel arch and N door and porch. The bullaun beside the path to the church is visited for wart cures.

O Davies in *Ulster J Archaeol* 2 (1939), 271-287 (dating requires revision); DOENI guide-card (1977); N F Brannon and B S Blades in *Ulster J Archaeol* 43 (1980), 91-96.

112 Gortycavan Mound (C791315)
3½ miles (5·6 km) WSW of Coleraine, on the E side of a minor road between the A2 and B201, one field from the road, on a ridge with extensive views NE to the Bann estuary. The mound, with a slightly dished summit, has traces of a bank round its edge and is surrounded by a ditch and outer bank. Though somewhat like a motte, it is likely to be in a pre-Norman raised rath or mound tradition. A mound in Big Glebe 2½ miles (4 km) NW, now levelled, was shown by excavation to be pre-Norman (awaiting publication). Gortycavan mound is heavily overgrown and awaits presentation (1982).

113 Inishrush Crannog (C937041)
2 miles (3·2 km) W of Portglenone, visible to the N of the minor road just W of Claudy RC church. The site of the crannog is marked by a small cluster of trees and bushes in the expanse of bog which is the partly-drained Green Lough. Earlier accounts suggest that the crannog was partly dismantled in the 19th century. The site cannot be safely approached across the bog: viewable only from the adjoining road.

W Reeves and W J Knowles in *Ulster J Archaeol* 10 (1904), 29-30 and 54.

114 Maghera Church (C855002)
On the E outskirts of the town in Largantogher townland near the approach by the A42. Parking near the graveyard gate and key available from the nearest house. St Lurach founded an important monastery here in the 6th century. It was plundered by Vikings in 832 and burned in 1135. Following the 12th-century ecclesiastical reforms this was the seat of a bishop from the mid 12th to the mid 13th century, then served as parish church until the new church across the road was built in the early 19th century. This long history is reflected in the much patched and altered fabric and the big uneven graveyard. The earliest part of the church is the nave, built of large, unevenly-sized stones and with traces of *antae*, perhaps as early as the 10th century. Of probably the mid 12th century is the fine W door, now under the added tower. Of the same structural type as the Banagher door,

with a lintel outside and a semicircular arch within, the outer face is elaborately carved with Romanesque decoration: interlace, floral and animal motifs on the jambs and a crowded crucifixion scene on the lintel, with Christ flanked by the thieves and eleven other figures (disciples?), and angels above the cross. The chancel may have been added in about 1200 and there are signs of later medieval and post-medieval alterations in the windows. The tower was probably added in the 17th century. W of the church, prominently sited in the graveyard, is a rough pillar stone with a carved ringed cross, visible only in good diagonal light. This is traditionally St Lurach's burial place. 52

O Davies in *Proc Belfast Nat Hist Phil Soc* 2 (1940-45), 17-22; Gwynn and Hadcock 1970, 93.

115 Mountsandel Fort (C853306) 122

1¼ miles (2 km) SSE of Coleraine, on the E bank of the river Bann in a forestry plantation, approached on foot by a forest path either from N or S. The large oval mound dominates the river and was clearly of great strategic importance, but its date remains something of a puzzle. Recent excavation in its vicinity has found nothing to support the traditional association of the mound with *Dún dá Beann*, an important Early Christian stronghold. It may be an earthwork fortification of the Anglo-Norman invasion period. The features on the mound's summit are difficult to interpret but a ring-work or

122 Mountsandel Fort from across the river Bann.

129

motte and bailey have both been suggested. The earthwork may have been used or modified for artillery warfare in the late 16th century or later. Only further excavation is likely to resolve these uncertainties.

T E McNeill, *Anglo-Norman Ulster* (Edinburgh, 1980), 103 and fig 2; P C Woodman's forthcoming report on Mount Sandel Mesolithic Site (no 105) (HMSO monograph) will include a report by A E P Collins on excavation at the edges of the mound.

116   Tullyheran Fort (C835017)
1¼ miles (2 km) NW of Maghera on the summit of a low hill in farm land. A well-preserved rath with a substantial inner bank enclosing the level interior, a wide ditch and an outer bank with an entrance gap to the SE.

PLANTATION PERIOD AND LATER MONUMENTS

117   Brackfield Bawn or Crossalt (C511096)
2½ miles (4 km) NW of Claudy, just N of the main A6 Londonderry road immediately S of Brackfield Presbyterian church. Large carpark at entrance. The bawn, sited on a hillslope, commands the ancient E-W route to Londonderry. It was built on land granted after the Flight of the Earls (1607) to the Skinners' Company and is shown in the drawing by Thomas Raven illustrating Sir Thomas Phillips's 1622 Survey. The rectangular walled bawn has egg-shaped flanker towers at opposite (N and S) corners, the S tower badly ruined. The position of the house along the SW wall of the enclosure is confirmed by surviving chimneys. There are gun-loops in the

123

123   Brackfield Bawn based on Thomas Raven's drawing.

130

flankers.

E M Jope in *Ulster J Archaeol* 23 (1960), 97-123.

118 Londonderry City Walls (C435167 and area) 124

The whole circuit of walls, enclosing the old city on the w bank of the river Foyle, is complete. Built for the Irish Society between 1613 and 1618, it underwent sieges in 1641, in 1648 and 1649, when the Parliamentarians held out against the Royalists and were relieved by General Owen Roe O'Neill, and in 1688-9 for 105 days against the forces of James II. An earthen rampart was faced with stone producing a wall 6–7·7 m high and 4·3-9·1 m wide, with a broad external ditch, now filled in. Five of the original eight artillery bastions survive and two shallow gun platforms. Two watch-towers are preserved near St Columb's Cathedral but all four original 125 gates have been changed: Bishop's Gate in 1789, commemorating the raising of the 1689 siege, and Butcher's, Ferryquay and Shipquay Gates in the 19th century. Three additional gates, Magazine, New and Castle Gates, are more recent. Twelve cannon are displayed on the N and W ramparts (40 originally defended the city) and others can be seen in Shipquay Street reused as bollards. The wall-top is reached by steps at several points inside the circuit. A recommended route would be to start at the N beside Shipquay Gate and move round in a clockwise direction. St Columb's Cathedral (1628-33) in the s angle of the walls is one of the most remarkable buildings of the Ulster Plantation.

C D Milligan, *The Walls of Derry, their building, defending and preserving* (Londonderry, 1948); HMSO guide-card (1969).

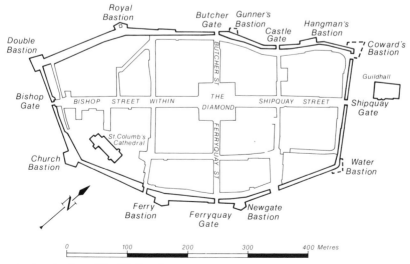

124 Londonderry City Walls, plan.

131

125   Londonderry, South Wall looking towards Bishop's Gate.

119   Magilligan Martello Tower (C660388)

In Doaghs Lower townland, 7 miles (11·2 km) WNW of Castlerock, reached by the lane to Magilligan Point. Martello towers were built round the Irish and English coasts between 1804 and 1812 to guard against Napoleonic

126   Magilligan Martello Tower early in this century.

invasion. Magilligan tower, built in 1812, together with another at Green-castle on the Donegal coast opposite, commanded the strategically important entrance to Lough Foyle. The circular tower is built of dressed stone, 10 m high, 12 m in diameter, tapering slightly upwards. The entrance at first floor level was by retractable ladder and the five-corbelled machicolation above gave added protection. The ground floor was a powder and ammunition store, the first was residential and on the top was a 24-pounder cannon on a central pivot and circular rail.

PLEASE NOTE: the tower is in Magilligan Nature Reserve (DOENI Conservation Branch) but visitors should take care not to stray onto the adjoining army ranges.

V J Enoch, *The Martello Towers of Ireland* (no date: 1978?); P M Kerrigan in *An Cosantóir* (July, 1982), 218-224.

120   Tirkane Sweat House (C827025)

2⅛ miles (3·4 km) NW of Maghera, ½ mile (0·8 km) W of Killelagh Lough, reached by a long path W from a by-road, with a lay-by at the roadside. The sweat house is set into the side of a small, leafy valley. Rectangular in plan, it is stone-built with a paved floor and lintelled roof. A small chimney hole allowed smoke to escape. The stone structure is covered with turf and looks externally like a grassy mound. It is difficult to date but may not be earlier than the 18th century. There is a small cold plunge bath nearby. The fine Neolithic dolmen in Tirnony townland is 1 mile (1·6 km) SE, easily accessible at the roadside.

PSAMNI (1940), 207; A Weir, *Early Ireland: a field guide* (Belfast, 1980), 80-81, 124.

County Tyrone

PREHISTORIC MONUMENTS

121   Balix Lower Court Grave: The White Rocks (H483963)
3 miles (4·8 km) N of Plumbridge, high on the E-facing hillside overlooking Butterlope Glen, in rough pasture. The valley still forms an important N-S route through the Sperrins. This court grave has a V-shaped forecourt at the uphill (W) end of a long cairn. The court opens into a chamber, now undivided but perhaps originally divided into two parts.

PSAMNI (1940), 216; F Lynch in *Ulster J Archaeol* 29 (1966), 39-42.

122   Ballywholan Dual Court Grave: Carnagat (H569470)
3½ miles (5·6 km) SE of Clogher, E of a minor road leading S off the B83, ½ mile (0·8 km) from the Monaghan border, in bogland overlooking the valley of the Fury river. Very well-preserved dual court grave in a long cairn. A semicircular forecourt at each end leads to two-chambered galleries. The site was partly excavated in 1899.

W Wulff in *J Roy Soc Antiq Ireland* 52 (1922), 38-41; *PSAMNI* (1940), 259.

123   Ballywholan Chambered Grave: Carnfadrig (H555490)
1½ miles (2·4 km) NW of no 122, on a hillslope N of the minor road which runs from the B83 S of Knockroe. A long, narrow cairn has at its E end a large chamber reached between two portal stones and over a sill. At the W end are two transversely set chambers. Like Carnagat, this cairn was partly excavated in 1899. Its name, Carnfadrig or Carnpatrick, comes from a traditional association with St Patrick, travelling along this valley from Armagh to Clogher.

W Wulff in *J Roy Soc Antiq Ireland* 53 (1923), 190-95 (but plan misleading); *PSAMNI* (1940), 258.

127
14
124   Beaghmore Stone Circles, Cairns and Alignments (H685842)
8½ miles (13·6 km) NW of Cookstown, on the SE fringe of the Sperrin Mountains, reached by minor roads N from the A505 Omagh road through Dunnamore, or from Draperstown SW by the Six Towns road. A large, impressive series of Bronze Age ceremonial stone monuments was excavated from the surrounding bog between 1945 and 1949 and in 1965. The main features are the stone circles (built of fairly small stones) occurring in

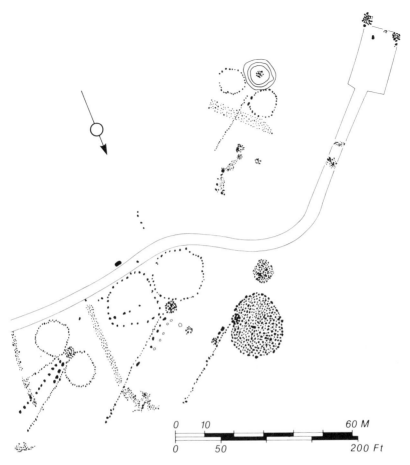

127   Beaghmore Stone Circles, Cairns and Alignments, plan.

pairs, with associated small cairns and stone alignments. The 'Dragon's Teeth' is a single large circle filled with closely-set stones. Running under these features are low banks of small stones, probably derived from clearing fields for arable farming in Neolithic times. Finds were sparse from the excavations but work on the pollen record suggests Neolithic activity from the mid 4th millennium BC, with the main period of the stone monuments in the Bronze Age – the late 2nd and early 1st millennia BC.

A McL May in *J Roy Soc Antiq Ireland* 83 (1953), 174-197; J R Pilcher in *Ulster J Archaeol* 32 (1969), 73-91; DOENI guide-card (with Cregganconroe) (1977).

125 Berrysfort Standing Stone (H272838)

⅔ mile (1·1 km) SE of Castlederg, approached by farm lanes and across a field. The tall (2·30 m high), shapely pillar stands on a small eminence, just S of the river Derg.

126 Churchtown Chambered Cairn: Todd's Den (H268856)

¾ mile (1·2 km) NNE of Castlederg, reached by a farm track E of the minor road which runs NNE from Castlederg to the Donegal border. Megalithic grave with large capstones apparently still in place, largely intact under its covering cairn. This is probably a wedge grave.

PSAMNI (1940), 220.

127 Churchtown Chambered Grave: Druid's Altar (H265854)

½ mile (0·8 km) NNE of Castlederg, on rising ground overlooking the valley of the river Derg, E of the same minor road as no 126. A single chamber remains, of massive stones, with one capstone in place and another collapsed. It is partly incorporated into, and confused by, a field wall.

PSAMNI (1940), 220.

128 Cregganconroe Court Grave (H663758)

3 miles (4·8 km) NW of Pomeroy, ½ mile (0·8 km) SSW of Cam Lough, best reached by a lane from the E. Park at the farmhouse and approach the site from the track left of the farm. On a prominent height in an area of sand and gravel ridges. A shallow forecourt at the E end opens between tall portal

128

128   Cregganconroe Court Grave.

136

stones (blocked by a fallen lintel) into a two-segment burial gallery. One huge slipped capstone survives. Further W in the rectangular cairn are two small lateral chambers, originally reached between portal stones from the long sides of the cairn. The site has not been excavated, in contrast to nearby Creggandevesky (no 129).

PSAMNI (1940), 237; DOENI guide-card (with Beaghmore) (1977).

129   Creggandevesky Court Grave (H643750)

2½ miles (4 km) NE of Carrickmore, prominently sited on a glacial hill at the W side of Lough Mallon. The recommended approach is on foot by the path round the S shore of the lough which leads off the minor road running NW from the B4 W of Pomeroy towards Creggan. Impressively well-preserved court grave, excavated between 1979 and 1982. A semicircular forecourt at the SE end leads to three burial chambers in a short trapezoidal cairn. The cairn's dry-stone side revetment walls still stand to some height and some of the roof corbel stones are still in place. Cremated bone, flint implements and Neolithic pottery were found during the excavation.

PSAMNI (1940), 238; publication by C Foley forthcoming.

130   Damphcloy Megalithic Structure (H595880)

In Crockatanty townland, 6½ miles (10·4 km) ENE of Gortin, remotely sited high on the E side of Greenan Hill, overlooking the valleys of the Owen-killew and its tributary, the Coneyglen Burn. A large slab supported at one side by the hillside and at the other by boulders has been taken to be a ruined portal grave, but it is unlikely to be an antiquity. It was probably a hillside shelter for people or stock.

PSAMNI (1940), 224.

131   Glenknock or Cloghogle Chambered Grave: Druid's Altar (H413879)

1½ miles (2·4 km) NNE of Newtownstewart, E of the minor road leading N off the B46 (Plumbridge) road at St Eugene's Church. The megalith is disturbed, but amongst the leaning stones it is possible to detect the broken capstone, one jamb and several side stones, and traces of a cairn. These are probably the remains of a portal grave or 'dolmen'.

PSAMNI (1940), 221.

132   Grange Standing Stone (H832748)

2¼ miles (3·6 km) SE of Cookstown, S of the hamlet of Grange, approached from the N along the side of a small graveyard and along the field boundary. A single, rather squat, standing stone.

133 Grange Standing Stones (H831752)

In a field N of Grange hamlet. A pair of standing stones about 6 m apart.

PSAMNI (1940), 240.

134 Killucan Chambered Grave: Carnanbane (H684795)

7¾ miles (12·4 km) W of Cookstown and S of Dunnamore, ½ mile (0·8 km) S of the main A505 Cookstown to Omagh road. Roughly circular cairn, augmented with field stones. Traces of a forecourt to the SW and of a two-segment burial gallery indicate a mutilated court grave.

PSAMNI (1940), 233.

135 Killucan Long Cairn: Killucan (H685801)

N of no 134, ⅛ mile (0·2 km) S of the A505. This may have been a court grave but it survives only as a confused long cairn with one large capstone at the E end.

PSAMNI (1940), 233.

136 Knockmany Passage Grave: Annia's Cove (H547559)

1¾ miles (2·8 km) NW of Augher, approached from Augher or Clogher, on the summit of Knockmany in the Forest Park, reached by an uphill path through the forest from the carpark on the NW side of the hill. The cairn commands superb views S over the Clogher Valley. The covering cairn in its present form is modern, added in 1959 to protect the stones from weathering and vandalism. Excavation showed that a stone cairn capped with earth within a stone revetment originally covered the burial chamber. The passage of the 'classic' passage grave is absent but the stones forming the chamber are decorated with characteristic passage grave art, including circles, spirals and zigzags – one of the best examples of this art in the north. There is access to the mound at all times, and a general view of the stones can be had through the gate of the chamber, but at time of writing there is no regular arrangement for unlocking the chamber. Prospective visitors who wish to examine the stones in detail should contact Historic Monuments and Buildings Branch to arrange for the chamber to be opened.

A E P Collins and D M Waterman in *Ulster J Archaeol* 15 (1952), 26-30; A E P Collins and H A Meek in *Ulster J Archaeol* 23 (1960), 2-8; guide book (HMSO, 1960).

137 Lisky Chambered Grave: Giant's Grave (H358904)

2 miles (3·2 km) SE of Sion Mills, S of the B165 Strabane to Newtownstewart road, on a rocky outcrop on the N bank of the river Mourne. A single long chamber is made up of six very large stones and may be the remains of a

court grave. Large stones in the vicinity may come from other chambers or from a court, but without excavation the original form is uncertain.

PSAMNI (1940), 217.

138   Tattykeel Standing Stone (H748774)
4 miles (6·4 km) W of Cookstown, S of the main A505 Cookstown to Omagh road and E of a farm track. A single shapely stone stands 2·15 m high.

129   Knockmany Passage Grave: late 19th-century view of decorated stone.

139

EARLY CHRISTIAN PERIOD MONUMENTS

139   Arboe Cross and Abbey (H966756)

In Farsnagh townland, 5 miles (8 km) ESE of Coagh, reached by turning S off the B73, on a promontory on the W shore of Lough Neagh. The tall cross marks the area of a monastery associated with St Colman, founded perhaps in the 6th century. Arboe was burned in 1166 but later emerged as the medieval parish church site. The cross is the finest of the Ulster figure-carved group, despite damage and weathering, with an exceptionally full scheme of biblical carving. On the E (Old Testament) side are Adam and Eve, the sacrifice of Isaac, Daniel between Lions, the Children in the Fiery Furnace, a figure with bell and crozier surrounded by people, and Christ in Glory with scales and flames beneath. The W (New Testament) side has the Visit of the Magi, the Miracle at Cana, the Multiplication of Loaves and Fishes, the Entry to Jerusalem, the Arrest and the Crucifixion. On the S side are Cain and Abel, David struggling with the Lion, David killing Goliath, and the raven feeding Paul and Anthony in the Egyptian desert. The scenes on the N side are less easy to interpret but the Baptism, the annointing of David, the Judgement of Solomon and the Slaughter of the Innocents have all been suggested. A 10th-century date is likely for the cross. Arboe 'Abbey' is a small, featureless ruin in the field N of the graveyard, overgrown and awaiting conservation (1982). The ruined church in the graveyard (not in State Care) lacks distinctive features but is probably of the early 17th century.

F J Bigger and W J Fennell in *Ulster J Archaeol* 4 (1897-8), 1-6; *PSAMNI* (1940), 241-2; H Roe in *Seanchas Ardmhacha* 2 no 1 (1956), 81-3.

140   Donaghmore Cross (H768654)

2½ miles (4 km) NW of Dungannon, at the busy road junction at the W end of Donaghmore's main street, outside the old graveyard. This sandstone cross survives from an early monastery on or near its present site, traditionally founded by St Patrick, who left the priest Colum there with book and bell. An Early Christian bronze bell associated with Donaghmore parish, known as the Bell of Clogher, is in the National Museum, Dublin. The church was later parochial. The present cross is made up of parts of two, the base and lower shaft not quite matching the upper shaft and head. It is known to have been thrown down in the 17th century and re-erected in the 18th. Its decoration includes an interesting mixture of figure-carving and motifs in distinctive circular, diamond-shaped and semicircular frames. On the E side are the Annunciation to the Shepherds, the Adoration of the Magi, the Miracle at Cana, the Multiplication of Loaves and Fishes, the Arrest and the Crucifixion. On the W side are Adam and Eve, Cain and Abel and the Sacrifice of Isaac. There is a horseman, perhaps unfinished, on the

140

130 Arboe Cross, west side.   *131 Donaghmore Cross, east side.*

w side of the base.

PSAMNI (1940), 245; H Roe in *Seanchas Ardmhacha* 2 no 1 (1956), 85-7.

141 Dungororan Rath (H738693)

5½ miles (8·8 km) NW of Dungannon, NE of the B43 to Pomeroy, approached by narrow farm lanes, prominently sited on a glacial hilltop. The rath is circular, its interior considerably raised, with traces of a low bank and a wide wet surrounding ditch.

142 Errigal Keerogue Cross and Church (H585570)

In Gort townland, 2¾ miles (4·4 km) w of Ballygawley, reached by minor roads N and NW from the A4 Ballygawley-Clogher road. The ridge-top graveyard is beautifully sited overlooking the Clogher valley. An early monastery associated with St Ciaran (Dachiarog) and the medieval parish church were here. The cross W of the church has been called 'archaic' and 'primitive', but it is clearly unfinished. On the E face a ringed cross is lightly II tooled; on the W a flat boss was worked and straight lines marked, but the stone was not further cut back, perhaps because of the flaw visible on the S side. Until recently the church was densely overgrown, but clearance and conservation have revealed opposed doors to N and S and a base batter on the E wall. Numerous querns and quern fragments have been found in the graveyard and a few are built for display into the N wall, together with a cast of a medieval burial monument found in the graveyard. St Kieran's Well is across the road to the NE.

PSAMNI (1940), 254; H Roe in *Seanchas Ardmhacha* 2 no 1 (1956), 88; N F Brannon in *Ulster J Archaeol* 44-45 (1981-2), 200-202.

143   Killyliss Rath (H757606)
2¾ miles (4·4 km) WSW of Dungannon, approached from the N by minor roads from the A4 (old main road). The rath has a very substantial bank, flanked by inner and outer ditches. Small-scale excavation done in 1965 is not yet published.

132   **144   Tullaghoge Fort** (H825743)
In Ballymully Glebe townland, 2½ miles (4·0 km) SSE of Cookstown, E of the B162 Cookstown to Stewartstown road. The entrance is on a difficult corner, with a small carpark at the foot of the hill, from which an uphill path leads to the site. This magnificent hilltop enclosure commands wide views and, planted with trees, is visible from miles around. The site comes into

132   Tullaghoge Fort, air view with Donaghrisk graveyard visible towards top right.

historical prominence in the 11th century when it was a dynastic centre and inauguration place of the Cenél nEógain (later the O'Neills). It was the residence of the O'Hagans who, with the O'Cahans, performed the inauguration ceremony. The O'Hagan burial place, Donaghrisk, is the circular walled graveyard at the foot of the hill to the sw. The earthwork is not of classic rath form. An inner polygonal embanked enclosure is separated from an outer bank by a wide, flat space. The fort is shown in Bartlett's 1601 pictorial map with two gateways and two thatched buildings, with the stone inauguration chair on the hillside to the SE. The chair was broken up by the English Lord Deputy Mountjoy, advancing N against the O'Neills in 1602. The work of clearing and presenting the site was done in 1964 with generous help from Mr J Tullyhogue O'Hagan.

Ulster J Archaeol 5 (1857), 235-42; Hayes-McCoy 1964, 8-9.

MEDIEVAL MONUMENTS

145 Harry Avery's Castle (H392852)   III
¾ mile (1·2 km) sw of Newtownstewart, approached across a field from the minor road to Rakelly. On a prominent hill commanding important river valley routes. The castle is named after Henry Aimbreidh O'Neill who died in 1392, but it is not certain whether it dates from the 14th or 15th century. It is an unusual and interesting ruin, a stone castle deep in Gaelic Ulster. An artificially scarped natural mound formed an elevated 'bailey' or courtyard, surrounded by a polygonal curtain wall, now ruined to a low level. At its sw end is a tower which *looks* like a gatehouse, entered between high D-shaped towers, but the only way into the courtyard behind was up a stair and through the hall at first floor level. In function the building resembles a tower-house rather than a true gatehouse. Features include a draw-bar slot for the main door, latrine chutes and marks of wicker centering in the tower vaults.

E M and H M Jope and E A Johnson in *Ulster J Archaeol* 13 (1951), 81-92; S G Rees-Jones and D M Waterman in *Ulster J Archaeol* 30 (1967), 76-82.

146 Magheraglass Church (H743767)
4¼ miles (6·8 km) wsw of Cookstown, difficult of access across fields. The overgrown remains of a ruined medieval church stand on the site of a pre-Norman church, its w wall incorporated into a field boundary. Not signposted or presented (1982).

H B Carter in *J Roy Soc Antiq Ireland* 23 (1893), 84-6; *PSAMNI* (1940), 239.

147 Mountjoy Castle (H901687)

In Magheralamfield townland, 3 miles (4·8 km) ESE of Stewartstown, reached by a lane W off the B161. Small carpark at entrance. Standing on a low hill overlooking Lough Neagh, the castle is a small early 17th-century campaign fort. The building is of stone below, with dressed quoins, and brick above, in parts badly weathered. The central rectangular block has four spear-shaped angle towers with gun-loops, but only the NE and SE towers are accessible to visitors. This is probably the fortification reported in 1611 by Sir George Carew as having been built 'beside the old fort' and finished by 1605. It is not to be identified with the large fort built by Francis Roe during Mountjoy's northward advance against O'Neill in 1602 and illustrated in a pictorial map by Richard Bartlett. This was probably on lower land closer to the lough shore. The forts in this area continued in use to the late 17th century.

E M Jope in *Ulster J Archaeol* 23 (1960), 97-125; Hayes-McCoy 1964, 13.

PLANTATION PERIOD AND LATER MONUMENTS

148 Benburb Castle (H814520)

In the grounds of Benburb Servite Priory, approached on foot down the drive from the main street beyond (w of) the main Priory entrance. Dramatically sited on the cliff edge above the river Blackwater, this is a bawn built

133 Benburb Castle from the east.

by Sir Richard Wingfield in about 1615, on or near the site of a stronghold of Shane O'Neill. The bawn walls enclose an irregular rectangular area, the walls standing almost to full height, plentifully supplied with gun-loops. At the NE and NW corners are rectangular towers, large, with fireplaces and more like tall houses than ordinary flankers. At the S end is a circular tower with a stair down to a postern gate at the cliff edge. The 19th-century house in the bawn is privately occupied. 133

PSAMNI (1940), 257; O Davies in *Ulster J Archaeol* 4 (1941), 31-4.

149 Castle Caulfield (or Caulfeild) (H755626) 134
In Lisnamonaghan townland, on the SE edge of the village. These are the substantial remains of an English-style house, built by Sir Toby Caulfield between 1611 and 1619 on the site of a fort of the O'Donnellys. The Caulfield arms appear over the gatehouse. This has murder-holes and pistol-loops and, with a fragment of bawn wall, is earlier than the main house. This was undefended, three storeys high with attics, and was originally of half H plan, but it is now L-shaped, lacking its NW wing. In the main block was a hall of medieval plan with opposed doorways, and the large windows in the NE gable suggest that the most important chambers were there. The kitchen was in the NE wing. The castle was burned by the O'Donnellys in 1641 but repaired and reoccupied by the Caulfields until the 1660s. There are still signs of the burning and plentiful evidence of structural alterations following the 1641 attack. St Oliver Plunkett is known to have held a service at the castle in 1670 and John Wesley preached there in 1767. The 17th-century parish church in the village has fine carved stonework, including some pieces said to be reused from the castle.

E M Jope in *Ulster J Archaeol* 21 (1958), 101-7.

134 Castle Caulfield, with gatehouse on the right.

150 Derryloran Church (H805768)

On the SW edge of Cookstown, beside the Ballinderry river, close to a bridge and on the A505 (Omagh) road. The ruined church probably occupies the site of a pre-Norman church associated with St Luran. A church here was plundered in 1195 and the medieval parish church was on this site. A 1622 survey reported a church as 'almost finished' and the present ruin seems to be of that church, though incorporating some earlier worked stones. The W porch was an 18th-century addition and the church was used until 1822. It is a long, narrow structure, well-supplied with windows including a three-light E window with uncusped intersecting tracery.

O Davies in *Ulster J Archaeol* 5 (1942), 8-11.

67, 68

151 Moy Gates and Screen (H851560)

On the N side of the road at the E approach to the Moy on the A29, these gates mark the entrance to the now-vanished Roxborough Castle. Between stone end-pillars are curving screens, openwork columns, and pedestrian and carriage gates, all of elaborate cast iron, the best surviving example of their type in Northern Ireland. Their exact date is uncertain, but they may be the work of the celebrated Dublin iron-founder, Richard Turner, who is known to have worked at Roxborough in the mid 19th century. This cast ironwork should be contrasted with the wrought iron Richhill Gates at
111 Hillsborough (no 86).

152 Reaskcor Tree-Ring (H749617)

3 miles (4·8 km) WSW of Dungannon, N of the A4, on a prominent hilltop with fine views. Though the spot is known as Fort Hill, this enclosure is not an Early Christian period rath but a 'tree-ring', a fairly slight circular bank, built probably in the 18th century, in which trees were planted. Most of the old trees have been felled here, but there are several other hilltop tree-rings in the area which retain their trees.

B B Williams in *Ulster J Archaeol* 43 (1980), 97-101 on tree-rings.

153 Reaskmore Penal Altar Site (H754586)

3½ miles (5·6 km) SW of Dungannon. A small, secluded space surrounded by bushes where Mass was celebrated during Penal times. Not signposted or presented.

154 Relignaman Women's Graveyard (H607722)

½ mile (0·8 km) SW of Carrickmore, on a rocky height with a large quarry to the E. A small, irregularly-shaped enclosure has a grass-grown tumbled wall and small, uninscribed stones and mounds marking graves. Traditionally only women were buried here: no dead man or living woman was meant to enter the enclosure. The monument in its present form is impossible to date closely (hence its inclusion in this section) but the use of the site may be very ancient. There was a pre-Norman church at Carrickmore and traditionally Relignaman originated from St Columba's insistence that a wicked woman should be buried out of earshot of his bell. At Carrickmore there were also special burial grounds for suicides, children and slain men.

G Gillespie in *J Roy Soc Antiq Ireland* 66 (1936), 295-311.

135   *Lurigethan Promontory Fort (Ant), air view (see p 148).*

Historic Monuments not in State Care: A Selected List

Many sites not in State Care were mentioned in the introduction but the detailed inventory has been confined to State Care monuments. The list which follows, arranged like the inventory by county and period, includes a small selection of others which are well worth visiting. It should be noted that raths are under-represented in the list, largely because of the problem of making a small selection from a very large number, and souterrains are omitted for safety reasons. Monuments after about 1650 are not normally included. Many of the sites are scheduled for protection under the Historic Monuments Act (NI) 1971 and a few are protected under Historic Buildings legislation of 1972.

Grid references are included to help in finding sites, but they vary in accessibility from monuments in always-open graveyards, on publicly-owned land or beside a public road, to others reached across farmland or high on a mountain. There is no right of access to most of these monuments and visitors are advised to seek the landowner's permission to approach a site on private property. The WARNING on page xii should also be noted.

COUNTY ANTRIM

Prehistoric Monuments
Carnanmore passage grave, East Torr and other townlands (D218388).
Carn Greine chambered grave, wedge grave, Craigarogan townland (J270843).
Ballymarlagh court grave (D140018).
Ballypatrick Forest dual court grave, on scenic drive, Glenmakeeran townland (D183352).
Browndod court grave (J205924).
Dunteige wedge grave (D323079).
28 Knock Dhu promontory fort, Ballyhackett and Linford townlands (D342066), possibly Early Christian.
Linford earthworks, not firmly dated but possibly prehistoric (D332072).
135 Lurigethan promontory fort, Knockans South townland (D225255), possibly Early Christian.
Lyles Hill, hilltop enclosure and cairn, Toberagnee townland (J248829).
Magheraboy passage grave (D037438).

148

Ticloy portal grave (D232118).
Tievebulliagh Neolithic axe factory (D193268).
White Park Bay burial mound (D023440).

Early Christian Period Monuments
Altagore cashel (D249349).
Armoy round tower (D078332).
Budore rath pair (J235762).
Dunmull, fortified rocky eminence, Toberdornan townland (C889370).
Dunseverick promontory fort (C988445).
Fair Head crannog in Lough na Cranagh, Cross townland (D178427).
Lisnalinchy rath (J299879).
MacArt's Fort, Ballyaghagan townland, on Cave Hill (J325796).
Rams Island round tower (J096721).
Rathmore, rath with added motte (J183873).
Tully rath group (J170793).
Turraloskin cross-carved pillar stone (D086381).

Medieval Monuments
Carrickfergus, St Nicholas's church (in use) (J414875).
Connor, 'Bishop's Castle', probable castle (J152969).
Crumlin (or Camlin) church, Ballydonaghy townland (J161767).
Culfeightrin church, Churchfield townland (D139398).
Donegore motte (J205879).
Doonbought castle (D108130).
Doonmore motte and bailey, Cross townland (D172426).
Dundermot motte (D061132).
Dunmurry motte (J289691).
Knockaholet motte and bailey (D049230).
Red Bay motte and bailey and stone tower (D243262).
Templastragh church and cross slab (D005442).

Plantation Period and later Monuments
Antrim parish church (in use) (J149865).
Ballygalley Castle, now part of a hotel (D373078).
Castle Chichester at Whitehead (J477921).
Craigagh Altar, Penal altar and enclosure, Inispollan townland (D231322).
Dunluce ruined church (C905409).
Galgorm ruined church (D082023).
Kilroot Bishop's Palace, house and bawn (J450895).
Lisburn Castle gate and walls, in Castle Garden (J270633).
St John's church (in use), Ballyharry townland on Island Magee (J464979).
Templecorran ruined church, Forthill townland, Ballycarry (J449938).

63

COUNTY ARMAGH

Prehistoric Monuments
Aghmakane, the Long Stones, megalith and cashel (J021252).
15   Ballard standing stone (J016234).
Dane's Cast linear earthwork, especially from H879389 in Killyfaddy townland to H884394 in Lisnadill townland.
20   Dorsey (or Dorsy) large earthwork enclosure (especially at H942189 and H953193).
King's Stables, Bronze Age ritual site, Tray townland (H838455).
Vicar's Cairn, Carnavanaghan townland (H914397).

Early Christian Period Monuments
32   Armagh: crosses at Cathedral (H874453) and ogham stone in Public Library nearby.
Cashel townland, hilltop cashel (H904367).
Corliss Fort, bivallate rath (H893168).
Eglish, two cross heads and one base in graveyard (H806502).
Legar Hill Fort, rath with added angle bastions for artillery, Corr and Dunavally townland (H848553).
27   Lisleitrim, trivallate rath with crannog in nearby lake (H903207).
Rathtrillick, trivallate rath (H757379).
Tynan, three crosses in Tynan Abbey grounds (the Terrace, Island and Well Crosses) (area of H758428).

Medieval Monuments
Armagh, St Patrick's Church of Ireland Cathedral (in use) (H874453).
Tullyard mound, probable motte (H874477).

Plantation Period and later monuments
Ballymoyer ruined church, Ballymyre townland (H964307).
Castleraw, castle and large earthwork enclosure (H927529).
Charlemont artillery fort (H854558).
Creevekeeran Castle (H785371).
Derrywarragh Island, the O'Connor Stronghold, tower and enclosure (H929643).

COUNTY DOWN

Prehistoric Monuments
Ballyalton court grave (J531447).
Ballybeen, the Long Stone, standing stone at Dundonald (J425730).

150

Barnmeen standing stone, Longstone Hill (J172330).
Dane's Cast linear earthwork, in Scarva demesne (J072432 and area), ½ mile (0·8 km) SE of Poyntz Pass (J068390 and area), and at Gamble's Bridge (J068365 and area).
Downpatrick hillfort (J482445).
Goward court grave (J237296).
Kempe Stones, portal grave, Greengraves townland (J445736).   6
Knockiveagh round cairn, Edenagarry townland (J182378).
Lappoges court grave (J256527).
Mayo standing stone, the Long Stone (J160266).
Portavoe standing stone (J572819).
Scrabo hilltop enclosure and hut circles (J478726).
Slidderyford Dolmen, portal grave, Wateresk townland (J394344).
Slieve Croob summit cairn (1755 feet), round cairn (J318454).

Early Christian Period Monuments
Ballyfounder rath (J621496).
Ballywillwill rath (J352415).
Castleskreen rath with added motte (J474403).
Castleskreen rath with added tower-house (J466400).
Donaghmore cross, in Church of Ireland churchyard, Glebe townland   35
(J104349).
Downpatrick cross east of Cathedral and others inside (J483445).
Drumbo round tower, in Presbyterian churchyard (J322651).
Dunbeg, small hillfort (not securely dated) (J339487).
Kilbroney cross and ruined (medieval) church (J187195).
Lough Brickland crannog (J111412).
Raholp church (J541479).
Rathmullan raised rath (J478373).,
Rathturret rath, Clonallan townland (J154189).
Saul mortuary house and cross slabs, in Church of Ireland church and graveyard (J509463).
Tara Fort, rath (J626485).
White Fort cashel, Drumaroad townland (J365440).

Medieval Monuments
Ardglass tower-houses: Cowd Castle (J561370), Margaret's Castle (J559369) and Ardglass Castle (J561371).
Ardkeen motte and bailey and church (J593571).
Ballymaghery motte (J223288).
Ballyroney motte and baileys (J216395).
Belvoir Park Mound, motte, Breda townland (J340698).
Castle Bright tower-house (J507383).
Crown Mound, motte and bailey, Sheeptown townland, Newry (J107279).

Donaghadee motte (J588801).

Downpatrick Cathedral (in use) (J482445).

Dromore urban tower-house (J202532).

Dundonald motte, Church Quarter townland (J418739).

Greencastle church and motte (J245118).

Holywood Priory, parish church, later friary, Ballykeel townland (J401795).

Killyleagh church (J524534).

Lismahon, mound on rath, Ballykinler Lower townland (J429389).

Magheralin church (medieval and 17th-century) (J128589).

Old Castle Ward, tower-house (J574499).

Ringhaddy church and tower-house (J539588).

Seafin Castle (J220388).

Walshestown Castle, tower-house and bawn (J545498).

Plantation Period and later Monuments

65   Bangor Customs House (in use), built in 1637 (J505822).

Donaghadee Church of Ireland parish church (in use) (J589798).

Killyleagh Castle (in use) and bawn, 17th-century and later (J523529).

Newtownards Market Cross, dated 1636 (J492741).

COUNTY FERMANAGH

Prehistoric Monuments

Aghanaglack dual court grave (H098436).

Annaghmore Glebe cairn kerb, at Wattle Bridge (H427201).

Ballyreagh dual court grave (H315504).

17   Boa Island, stone figures in Caldragh graveyard, Dreenan townland (H085620).

Coolbuck wedge grave (H310439).

Killy Beg wedge graves (G982542).

Kilrooskagh portal grave (H061400).

Kiltierney passage grave (H217627).

Moylehid passage grave on Belmore Mountain (H150416).

Moylehid ring cairn (H151415).

Reyfad decorated stones (H112461).

Sheehinny round cairns, on Knockninny (H273302 and H275303).

Topped Mountain round cairn, Mullyknock townland (H311457).

Early Christian Period Monuments

36   Boho cross, Toneel North townland (H112462).

Carrick Lough crannog, Largalinny townland (H095540).

Cornashee mound and enclosures, in part perhaps prehistoric (H367348).

Galloon, two cross shafts in graveyard (H391227).
Golan rath (H438303).
Killadeas figure-carved stone and cross slab, Rockfield townland 38
(H206540).
Killykeeghan cashel (H109342).
Lisnaskea cross in market (H364340).
Rahallan rath (H150398).

Medieval Monuments
Aghamore or Carrick church (H096539).
Davy's Island church (H174593).
Derrybrusk church, Fyagh townland (H277391).
Kinawley church, Lismonaghan townland (H229308).   59
Templenaffrin church (H102388).
Templerushin church at Holywell, Rushin townland (H076397).
Tievealough church (G978598).

Plantation Period and later Monuments
Aghalane Castle, bawn, Killycloghan townland (H341200).
Braade sweat house, in Lough Navar Forest Park (H055546).
Corratrasna, remains of early 17th-century gabled house (H279301).
Crevinish Castle, house and bawn (H165626).
Derrygonnelly church (H120524).   60
Enniskillen, remains of artillery fort on Fort Hill (H239442).
Enniskillen, St Macartan's Cathedral, 17th-century tower, monuments and
font (H234443).
Old Castle Caldwell, Plantation castle with gothick additions (H018605).
Portora Castle, house and bawn (H223454).

COUNTY LONDONDERRY

Prehistoric Monuments
Altibrian round cairn (C745299).
Ballydullaghan multiple cist cairn, Cornaclery (C836113).
Boviel wedge grave, Cloghnagalla (C730078).   10, 11
Carrick East chambered grave (C704174).
Clagan standing stones (C582055).
Cregg standing stone, the White Stone (C533080).
Crevolea chambered grave (C847233).
Drumderg chambered grave, Dergmore's Grave (H750960).
Glasakeeran wedge grave (C571151).
Gortcorbies round cairns (C741259 and area).
Knockoneill complex cairn, Tamnybrack (C819087).
Largantea wedge grave, Well Glass Spring Cairn (C726268).

Moneydig portal grave in cairn, the Daff Stone (C889165).
Tamlaght (Coagh) portal grave, Cloghtogle (H887790).
Tamnyrankin court grave (C838100).
Tireighter wedge grave (C590019).
Tirnony Dolmen, chambered grave (C841017).

Early Christian Period Monuments
Ballyhacket Lisawilling mound (C749331).
Camus cross and bullaun stone in graveyard (C871289).
Cashel townland, White Fort cashel (C719068).
Drumceatt mound, Mullagh townland, Daisy Hill (C666216).
Dunglady multivallate rath (C897040).
Giants Sconce, fortified rocky height (C772298).
Lough Enagh crannog in Lough Enagh East (C471194).
Mullaboy cross, in Roman Catholic graveyard (C512139).
Rough Fort rath, Limavady, Moneyrannel townland (C663229).
Tullybrisland cross (C560209).

Medieval Monuments
Ballycairn motte and bailey (C834342).
Ballynascreen church, Moneyconey townland (H730907).
Ballywillin church, Glebe townland (C870386).
Church Island, Lough Beg, church and bullaun stone (H974946).
Doherty Tower, Elagh More townland (C415216).
Drumachose church, Fruithill townland (C693231).
Enagh church, Templetown townland (C468195).
Faughanvale church (C580209).
Mill Loughan mound, probable motte (C875291).
Tamlaghtard church, saint's grave and holy well (C678313).

Plantation Period and later Monuments
Ballydonegan sweat house (C628024).
Ballykelly ruined church, near Walworth Bawn (C623227).
Bellaghy Bawn (in use) (H953963).
Culmore fort and earthwork (C477224).
Movanagher Bawn (C920159).
Salters' Castle, house and bawn (H953824).
Walworth Bawn, Ballykelly, house and bawn (in use) (C625227).

COUNTY TYRONE

Prehistoric Monuments
Aghagogan wedge grave and standing stone (H640736).

Aghalane court grave (H547786).
Altdrumman portal grave (H578768).
Altmore alias Barracktown court graves (H668696).
Athenree portal grave (H627715).
Ballyrenan chambered grave (H373832).
Clady Haliday court grave (H342886).
Clare court grave (H591739).
Clogher hillfort, prehistoric and Early Christian (H539514).
Clogherny wedge grave and stone circle (H488945).
Copney stone circles (H599770).
Davagh Lower wedge grave (H701871), ring cairn and alignment
    (H708868) in Davagh Forest Park.
Dunnamore wedge grave (H685809).
Dun Ruadh multiple cist cairn, Crouck townland (H623845).
Findermore, Abbey Stone, standing stone with added cross (H517511).
Leitrim portal grave (H226800).
Loughash wedge grave (C843009).
Loughmacrory wedge grave (H586776).   11
Loughmacrory court grave (H585770).
Loughry wedge grave (H812749).
Murnells portal grave in long cairn (H680757).
Radergan chambered grave (H555644).
Sess Kilgreen passage grave (H604584).
Sess Kilgreen decorated stone (H603585).
Tremoge stone circles (H654733).

Early Christian Period Monuments
Aghascrebagh ogham stone (H618839).   33
Ballynabwee rath (C409050).
Caledon cross, Demesne townland (H753437).
Clogher, sundial in Cathedral and crosses in graveyard (H537516).
Clonfeacle cross, in graveyard of Roman Catholic church, Tullydowey
    townland (H838520).
Dunmisk hilltop rath (H627707).
Edenageeragh rath (H696524).
Gortalowry rath, Cookstown (H809774).
Killoan, the Headstone, cross base (H297753).
Leitrim cashel (H221802).
Lough Fea mound (possibly medieval) (H761866).
Mullaghmore rath (H783649).
Mullaghslin rath (H563726).
Roughan crannog, in Roughan Lough (H828687).
Sessiamagaroll rath with added mound, perhaps motte (H812540).
Sixmilecross rath (H568676).

Medieval Monuments

Cappagh church (partly post-Plantation), Dunmullan townland (H450802).

Corickmore Abbey, Third Order Franciscan friary church (H452881).

Donaghedy old church, Bunowen townland (C454045).

Plantation Period and later Monuments

Aghaloo ruined church, Rousky townland (H663549).

Aghintain (Aughentaine) Castle (H499514).

Altadaven, St Patrick's Well and Chair and bullauns (H494523).

Ballyclog ruined church, Glebe townland (H866737).

Benburb, Clonfeacle Church of Ireland parish church (in use) (H817522).

Cadian sweat house (H768556).

Carnteel ruined church (H694546).

Castlecaulfield, Donaghmore Church of Ireland parish church (in use) (H755629).

Castle Curlews, Kirlish townland (H319758).

Castlederg Castle, bawn, Castlesessagh townland (H260844).

Derrywoone Castle, Barons Court townland (H366836).

Favor Royal bawn, Lismore townland (H631538).

Newtown Stewart Castle (H402858).

62 Roughan Castle (H823683).

Spur Royal Castle (in use), Augher, Castlehill Demesne townland (H561538).

Suggestions for Further Reading

Individual site references already given in the inventory entries are not usually repeated here. This list contains a selection of general works and books and articles on periods and types, with the same emphasis as in the book as a whole, on field monuments and buildings. Whilst *Ulster J Archaeol* is the main vehicle for archaeological articles, other publications in which archaeological material sometimes appears include *Ulster Local Studies*, the *Bulletin of the Ulster Place-Name Society*, the many Ulster local historical society journals and the lists and monographs of the Ulster Architectural Heritage Society. Past and present editions of the Ordnance Survey 6 inch and 1:10,000 series maps provide an invaluable store of information about field monuments, while the 1 inch and 1:50,000 maps are useful for locating the major sites.

GENERAL

An archaeological survey of county Down (HMSO, Belfast, 1966).

D A CHART (ed), *A preliminary survey of the ancient monuments of Northern Ireland* (HMSO, Belfast, 1940).

M CRAIG, *The architecture of Ireland* (London, 1982).

H DIXON, *An introduction to Ulster architecture* (Belfast, 1975).

E E EVANS, *Prehistoric and Early Christian Ireland: a guide* (London, 1966).

LORD KILLANIN AND M DUIGNAN, *The Shell Guide to Ireland* (London, 1969).

F MITCHELL, *The Irish landscape* (London, 1976).

E R NORMAN AND J K S ST JOSEPH, *The early development of Irish society: the evidence of aerial photography* (Cambridge, 1969).

S P Ó RÍORDÁIN, *Antiquities of the Irish countryside* (revised edition by R de Valera, London, 1979).

A ROWAN, *North West Ulster* (The Buildings of Ireland series, 1979).

A WEIR, *Early Ireland: a field guide* (Belfast, 1980).

PREHISTORIC

A M ApSimon, 'The earlier Bronze Age in the north of Ireland', *Ulster J Archaeol* 32 (1969), 28-72.

D Bateson, 'Roman material from Ireland: a reconsideration', *Proc Roy Irish Acad* 73C (1973), 21-97.

W C Borlase, *The dolmens of Ireland*, 3 vols (London, 1897).

A Burl, *The stone circles of the British Isles* (Yale, 1976).

H Case, 'Settlement-patterns in the north Irish Neolithic', *Ulster J Archaeol* 32 (1969), 3-27.

O Davies, 'Stone circles in Northern Ireland', *Ulster J Archaeol* 2 (1939), 2-14.

E E Evans, *Lyles Hill: a late Neolithic site in county Antrim* (HMSO, Belfast, 1953).

L N W Flanagan, *Ulster* (Heinemann Regional Archaeologies, London, 1970).

M Herity, *Irish passage graves* (Dublin, 1974).

M Herity and G Eogan, *Ireland in prehistory* (London, 1977) (very extensive bibliography).

C J Lynn, 'The Dorsey and other linear earthworks', in *Studies on early Ireland*, ed B G Scott (Belfast, 1982), 121-128.

B Raftery, 'Irish hill-forts', in *The Iron Age in the Irish Sea Province*, ed C Thomas (London, 1972).

A Ross, *Pagan Celtic Britain* (London, 1967).

E Shee-Twohig, *The megalithic art of western Europe* (Oxford, 1981).

R de Valera, 'The court cairns of Ireland', *Proc Roy Irish Acad* 60C (1959-60), 9-140.

P C Woodman, *The Mesolithic in Ireland* (British Archaeological Reports, Oxford, 1978).

EARLY CHRISTIAN PERIOD

M G L Baillie, *Tree-ring dating and archaeology* (London, 1982) for crannogs and mills.

A E P Collins, 'Settlement in Ulster, 0-1100 AD', *Ulster J Archaeol* 31 (1968), 53-58.

F Henry, *Irish Art in the Early Christian period to 800* (1965), *during the Viking invasions* (1967), and *in the Romanesque period* (1970) (all London).

——————— *Irish high crosses* (Dublin, 1964).

H Hickey, *Images of stone: figure sculpture of the Lough Erne basin* (Belfast, 1976).

K Hughes and A Hamlin, *The modern traveller to the early Irish church* (London, 1977), reprinted as *Celtic monasticism* (New York, 1981).

H G Leask, *Irish churches and monastic buildings*, vol 1 *the first phases and the Romanesque* (Dundalk, 1955).

C J Lynn, 'The excavation of Rathmullan, a raised rath and motte in county Down', *Ulster J Archaeol* 44-45 (1981-82), 65-171.

R A S Macalister, *Corpus Inscriptionum Insularum Celticarum*, 2 vols (Dublin, 1945 and 1949).

M and L de Paor, *Early Christian Ireland* (London, 1978).

V B Proudfoot, 'The economy of the Irish rath', *Medieval Archaeology* 5 (1961), 94-122.

——————, 'Irish raths and cashels: some notes on chronology, origins and survivals', *Ulster J Archaeol* 33 (1970), 37-48.

H M Roe, 'The high crosses of county Armagh' and 'The high crosses of east Tyrone', in *Seanchas Ardmhacha* 1 no 2 (1955) and 2 no 1 (1956).

R Warner, 'The Irish souterrains and their background' in *Subterranean Britain*, ed H Crawford (London, 1979), 100-144.

MEDIEVAL

A Gwynn and R N Hadcock, *Medieval religious houses: Ireland* (London, 1970).

H G Leask, *Irish churches and monastic buildings*, vol 2 *Gothic architecture to A.D. 1400* and vol 3 *Medieval Gothic, the last phases* (Dundalk, 1960).

H G Leask, *Irish castles* (Dundalk, 1964).

T E McNeill, 'Ulster mottes, a checklist', *Ulster J Archaeol* 38 (1975), 49-56.

——————, *Anglo-Norman Ulster: the history and archaeology of an Irish barony, 1177-1400* (Edinburgh, 1980).

R A Stalley, *Architecture and sculpture in Ireland 1150-1350* (Dublin, 1971).

159

POST-MEDIEVAL

R Buchanan, 'Corbelled structures in Lecale, county Down', *Ulster J Archaeol* 19 (1956), 92-112.

G Camblin, *The town in Ulster* (Belfast, 1951).

M Gowen, '17th century artillery forts in Ulster', *Clogher Record* 10 no 2 (1980), 239-257.

E R R Green, *The industrial archaeology of county Down* (HMSO, Belfast, 1963).

G A Hayes-McCoy, *Ulster and other Irish maps c. 1600* (Dublin, 1964).

E M Jope, 'Scottish influences in the north of Ireland: castles with Scottish features, 1580-1640', *Ulster J Archaeol* 14 (1951), 31-47.

——————, 'Moyry, Charlemont, Castleraw and Richhill: fortification to architecture in the north of Ireland', *Ulster J Archaeol* 23 (1960), 97-123.

W A McCutcheon, *The industrial archaeology of Northern Ireland* (HMSO, Belfast, 1980).

P Robinson, 'Vernacular housing in Ulster in the seventeenth century', *Ulster Folklife* 25 (1979), 1-28.

A Weir, 'Sweathouses and simple stone structures in county Louth and elsewhere in Ireland', *Co Louth Archaeol J* 19 no 3 (1979), 185-196.

Index

162